CHINESE DRESS

VERITY WILSON

PHOTOGRAPHS
BY IAN THOMAS

VICTORIA AND ALBERT MUSEUM • FAR EASTERN SERIES

First published by the
Victoria and Albert Museum,
London, 1986
Reprinted 1990 in paperback in England by Bamboo Publishing Ltd
and in Hong Kong by Oxford University Press in association with
the Victoria and Albert Museum
Reprinted 1996 in paperback by the Victoria and Albert Museum
Second reprint 1998

The Victoria and Albert Museum
London SW7 2RL

ISBN 1 85177 184 0

A catalogue record for this book is available from the British Library

Front cover illustration: Manchu woman's robe, embroidery in
twill weave silk, 19th century
Back cover: Detail of embroidery on the above robe

Book design by Morrison Dalley Design Partnership
Cover design by Mariana Canelo
Line illustrations by Paul Sharp
Printed in Singapore by Toppan Printing Co Ltd

Contents

Acknowledgements

All present and many past members of the Far Eastern Department of the Victoria and Albert Museum helped with this book in different ways. Several members of the Department of Textiles and Dress made useful comments on the manuscript. Margaret Dobbie of the Textile Conservation Department gave much technical information and, along with other members of that department, prepared the objects for photography. Graham Martin carried out X-ray fluorescence analysis on examples of gold thread and metal buttons. The staff of the Bethnal Green Museum of Childhood made available the Door of Hope Mission dolls for study and photography. I am also grateful to Professor Jonathan Spence for permission to quote from his book *Emperor of China: Self-portrait of K'ang-Hsi,* and to the heirs of Edward Brenan for allowing us to use his photograph.

Note on Spelling and Pronunciation

The *pinyin* system of romanising the Chinese script is used throughout, following the spelling given in *Xinhua Zidian*, revised edition (Peking, 1971). The only exceptions are Chinese terms and proper names within quotations, which are left in their original form, and the place names Peking, Canton and Hong Kong. Since no agreed standard exists governing word division in romanised Chinese, the grouping of characters has been left to individual authors to carry out as seems appropriate in individual cases.

The following few hints may help the reader unfamiliar with the system at least to pronounce words to themselves:
    Initial *zh-*, as English *j-*
    Initial *x-*, as English *s-*
    Initial *c-*, as English *ts-*
    Initial *q-*, as English *ch-*

Note on Measurements

Unless otherwise stated the first measurement is the vertical measurement and the second the horizontal measurement. All garments were measured down the back seam from neck to hem and across the shoulders from cuff to cuff.

Introduction

The first item of Chinese dress to enter the collection of the Victoria and Albert Museum was acquired in 1863 and is believed to be contemporary with its purchase date. The most recent acquisition, a post-1949 traditional-style padded suit, was included in a generous bequest of textiles left to the Museum in 1983 by Sir John Addis along with his collection of Chinese furniture. Out of a total of some two hundred and fifty garments the vast majority are from the eighteenth, nineteenth and twentieth centuries and nearly all of them were worn by that small minority of Chinese which possessed money and prestige. Few of the styles are worn by Chinese today although in some instances the garment cut and button and loop fastenings of earlier times persist.

No attempt to impose a rigid classification on the entire dress tradition of Qing dynasty China (1644-1911) has been entirely successful. The varied nature of the surviving examples cannot easily be reduced to a few categories. Not only the extant objects but also the evidence of Chinese literature and the reports of western travellers illustrate the blurred nature of the boundaries between these categories, and show that the use of clothing owed at least as much to personal status and individual taste as it did to centrally imposed regulations. For an account based on these prescriptive sources, which must not be entirely neglected, the reader is referred to the works of Schuyler Cammann detailed in the notes. Such regulations, which have been analysed by a number of authors, seem unlikely to yield further understanding of the subject and it is necessary, while absorbing what they have to tell us, to turn to the surviving garments.

This book is therefore written around the Museum's collection. It does not seek to be a complete history of Chinese dress. The first chapter deals with dragon robes and court robes and although both of these garment types were, on certain occasions, worn by the emperors the text makes clear their much wider usage outside court circles. Other dress styles are described in the second chapter. The concept 'dress' is here expanded to include such cultural phenomena as jewellery, hairstyles and make-up, all of which play an equally important part in the presentation of the self to the world. One of the chief points of reference in the Chinese garment tradition is not, as with many other cultures, the actual form of the human body but is the surface of the fabric, a surface which provides a field for a representation of the wearer's status and aspirations through formal patterning. This patterning, the effectiveness of which at its very best has been eloquently described by Ernst Gombrich, has enhanced the garments' attractiveness in the eyes of western connoisseurs. However, a concentration on the categorization of patterning has perhaps regrettably led to a lack of critical thought about technical and aesthetic features. Many robes in the Museum's collection show stereotyped design and casual execution.

In the third chapter are treated some aspects of dress technology. Dye materials and weave analysis are not included in this study. While it is known in outline what dyestuffs were used in East Asia, their application to individual items of clothing in the collection has not yet been ascertained. The production of cloth is only the first stage in the making of a wearable garment. Apart from those robes which were shaped on the loom, the weaver did not necessarily know to what final use a particular bolt of cloth would be put. In order for the story of Chinese dress as opposed to textiles to be carried forward a discussion of the highly complex weave structures is deferred.

The overriding importance hitherto attached to dating in the study of the applied arts and of Chinese dress in particular is explicitly brought into question in the final chapter of this book. The present study does not seek to provide a still more refined scheme of dating but to open up the subject in areas which have been relatively less well explored.

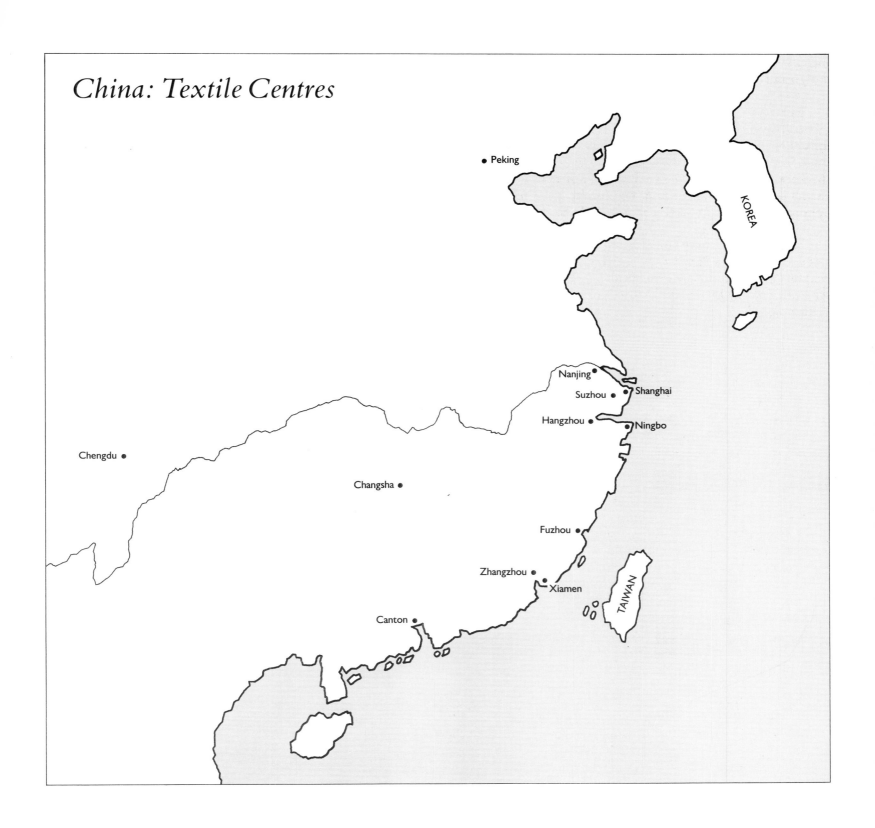

Official and Court Dress

Dragon Robes and Their Wearers

1 A remarkable oil painting in the Victoria and Albert Museum depicting Queen Victoria opening the Great Exhibition in 1851 shows, unmistakable among the foreign ambassadors, a Chinese visitor. He is wearing the kind of garment which has passed into the consciousness of English-speaking curators and collectors as a 2 'mandarin robe' or a 'dragon robe'. The dragon robe, in Chinese *long pao,* the term favoured by contemporary Chinese scholars, is typified by plate 2. [1] *Long pao* are mostly blue, but brown, turquoise, orange, yellow and red ones do exist and were predominantly worn by men. Women possessed garments which exhibited some similarities. The salient features are the hem design of stripes representing water with turbulent waves above, repeated on the sleeves at elbow level, and mountain peaks rising from the water, with symmetrically–placed dragons among clouds covering the main body of the garment. The cut too is one commonly associated with dragon robes. Arbitrarily taking this as the norm, we must bear in mind the existence of numerous variants. Indeed, the robes worn by the Chinese visitor lack certain supposedly standard features. The longer of the two robes does not have the 'standing water' design at the hem. Reality at once appears more confusing than orderly. In the course of this book it will become obvious that garments of many types worn by both sexes have a broad resemblance to dragon robes. Dragon robes exist in western collections in huge numbers, and this alone should alert us to their commonplace nature.

Who wore these robes? Though their major associations are with male members of the Chinese bureaucracy, it is not frivolous to start by pointing out that in the nineteenth and twentieth centuries at least some of them were worn by Europeans as dressing gowns. They probably found their way to the West through the agency of such firms as Liberty & Co. in Regent Street, London. [2] There exists in the Museum's collection an example tailored for this very purpose (12-1881). George Smith's melodramatic painting 'The Rightful Heir', exhibited at the Royal Academy in 1874, depicts the wicked usurper clearly wearing a dragon robe. [3] This angry Victorian is as far as he can be from the dignified mandarin of popular imagination, and we may assume that he was not unique in his choice of clothes. It seems likely that garments in this traditional pattern continued to be manufactured well into the twentieth century, long after they had ceased to have any function in Chinese society, purely for sale to western tourists.

Even within China, some foreign males had legitimate reasons for appropriating dragon robes as part of the full-dress apparel of the Chinese élite. The large body of Catholic missionaries enjoyed the right to wear them as did the European senior staff of the Imperial Chinese Maritime Customs established in 1854. [4] Edward

3 Brenan, just such a customs official, was granted the right to wear the insignia of the First Class of the Third Division of the Imperial Chinese Order of the Double Dragon on 18 December 1908. As well as the official document confirming the award, Mr Brenan's heirs have an account, written in English, of the cost of the entire ensemble. Many other Europeans were given official rank as a gesture of thanks or courtesy. Reginald Johnston, tutor to the last boy emperor, records in his *Twilight in the Forbidden City* that he was honoured in this way in 1922.[5] Professor W.E. Soothill, on leaving his post at a university in Shaanxi province at the beginning of the twentieth century, provides another example of a westerner presented with Chinese official credentials. We do not know if either of these two gentlemen ever owned or wore the robes they were entitled to, only that Professor Soothill's small son was given 'an official hat for when he became a mandarin'.[6]

Turning to the Chinese population, there are many instances in the Qing period (1644–1911) of dragon robes being worn without any of the accessories often thought to be essential to such garments. A photograph taken by M. Miller in Canton between 1861 and 1864 shows a group of three translators. The garment worn by one of them is a dragon robe caught in at the waist with a narrow belt and reaching to just below his ankles. Although the length varied according to the fashion of the moment, Chinese dress for both sexes never swept the ground. The vanity of Yehonala (1834–1908), the formidable female ruler better known by her title of Dowager Empress Cixi, outweighed any feelings she may have had about

Below left:
1 *The Opening of the Great Exhibition, 1851*, by Henry Selous, oil on canvas, 169 × 249 cm, 329–1889.

Below right:
3 *Edward Brenan*, a Deputy Commissioner in the Imperial Chinese Maritime Customs wearing dragon robe insignia, c. 1908.

13

the sanctity of court life. One of the photographs taken by her court photographer between 1902 and 1908 shows her being carried in her chair and attended by eunuchs in dragon robes without overgarments.[7]

Holders of official rank in the Chinese bureaucracy were distinguished as members of the government élite not so much by their dragon robes as by the other garments worn with them. The Chinese inscription on the watercolour illustrated here and dated to around 1795 tells us that the gentleman is a fourth rank official. The striped hem decoration and turned back cuffs are the only visible parts of his

4 dragon robe, the rest being hidden beneath a plain, dark, front-fastening coat, in Chinese called a *pu fu*. His square badge of office is applied to the back and front of this outer coat while round his neck is fastened a detachable stiffened collar over which is a long string of beads. He wears thick-soled boots and a spiked and fringed hat. Mrs Archibald Little, a European woman living in China in the 1880s and an entertaining and copious writer on the country, records in her book *Intimate China* her meeting with a Chinese general. Her description of him illustrates the range of accessories that might be worn by a high-ranking official:

> 'who was over six feet one, and fully broad in proportion, and who presented a most gorgeous appearance in long brocade gown embroidered for about a foot round the bottom with waves of the sea and other Chinese devices. He wore also a breast plate, and a similar square of embroidery on the back, with the horse-shoe cuffs... falling over his hands. High official boots, an amber necklace of very large beads reaching to his waist, and aureole-shaped official cap with large red tassel, completed his costume'.[8]

5 Except for the hat the costume in a photograph illustrated here fits Mrs Little's description quite closely. Taken in a studio in Rangoon, Burma around the turn of this century, it entered the Museum's collection as showing a 'military mandarin (Admiral)'. Military officials 'breast plates' displayed animal insignia, while those of civil officers carried a bird design.[9]

Legitimate government servants, like Mrs Little's general, and the Victoria and Albert Museum's admiral and fourth rank bureaucrat, would undoubtedly have passed through the Chinese examination system, obtained rank, and secured a post by virtue of their comfortably-off family backgrounds which provided them with access to education when young and useful contacts later on. The vast majority of imperial employees would have had little, if anything, to do with court life in Peking, most of them slotting into the network of local government posts throughout China. It was in these various capacities that they would have worn their full dragon robe ensemble when carrying out their official business as magistrates or tax collectors to give two examples.

We can be sure that custom in the matter of official dress varied from place to place and from time to time. *Politesse Chinoise* (1906), a handbook of Chinese etiquette for Catholic missionaries in China, the author of which was himself Chinese, admits confusion over certain points of dress.[10] However, we should not underestimate the authority and influence inherent in these dragon-decorated garments. Shen Fu, a poor but genteel early nineteenth century writer, has left us a

Opposite:
2 *Dragon robe*, embroidery on twill weave silk, late 19th century, 142 × 164 cm, T.219-1948.

14

府廣品四

4 *Official of the Fourth Rank*, watercolour on
  paper, c. 1795, from a volume
  19.2 × 11 cm, D. 898-1898.

5 *Military official*, photograph taken in a
  Rangoon studio, c. 1900.

16

rare autobiographical sketch, *Six Records of a Floating Life,* in which he tells us how the monks of a temple he wanted to visit would not receive him because he was not dressed as a government official. [11] A European writer recalls a Chinese governor who, when faced with a riotous mob during the unsettled period following the 1911 Revolution donned his full robes of office. The appearance of a robed official at a time when China had just overthrown the emperor seems likely to have been an unwise move but we are not told the consequences. [12]

It was also sometimes possible to buy the prestige associated with these garments. In the mid–nineteenth century, the government bestowed rank, and on occasion actual office, on rich men who were prepared to give financial assistance to the suppression of anti-government rebels and there is earlier evidence of rank buying. [13] The portrait of Wu Bingjian (1769-1843) or 'Howqua' as he was known to the foreign community in Canton, shows this merchant, albeit an influential merchant, wearing the costume of a man of rank. His dragon robe is predominantly green, a colour not represented in the Museum's collection, while the lower sleeve, also green and just visible on the right hand side of the painting, displays the characteristic tucking. The cuffs are worn turned back to display the fur facing and the outer coat is opulently lined throughout with a contrasting fur. He is hatless and does not wear a flaring collar. Howqua's luxurious appearance would suggest that considerable sums of money could be paid for such an outfit and Lady Hosie, an Englishwoman born in China and returning there to teach at the beginning of the twentieth century, mentions cost as an inhibiting factor in taking up office. The father of one of her Chinese acquaintances had to remain out of office because of the expense. [14] Li Ciming, a late nineteenth century official, on first taking up his appointment could not afford a full set of official robes and borrowed the garments from the family in which he was a tutor. [15] Dragon robes were on occasion worn even by the successive emperors of Qing China. Pictorial representations exist showing several rulers in such garments. [16]

6 *Portrait of the merchant Wu Bingjian (Howqua)*, watercolour on paper, c.1840-1850, 24.8 × 18.9 cm, E.816-1937.

Decorative Motifs of the Dragon Robe

The pattern elements and the shape of the dragon robe are its two most distinctive features. Because of the lack of extant early costume, it is not now possible for us to state categorically when certain Chinese decorative motifs were first used on items of Chinese dress and we have to turn to objects in other materials to identify the origins of eighteenth and nineteenth century dress designs. The water, mountain, cloud and dragon combination on the robe illustrated makes at least one early appearance at the Buddhist temple complex of Dunhuang in north-west China on a wall-painting in Cave 130 datable to the Tang dynasty (618-906) and the same design is frequently seen on ceramics and lacquer of the Ming period (1368-1644). The nine golden dragons on this robe – three on both the front and the back, one on each shoulder, and one on the hidden inside section – are five-clawed, a type, according to some writers, reserved for the emperor and his immediate family.

While this may have been so for earlier centuries, the large number of five-clawed dragons and the inferior quality of many of the robes and other objects on which they appear clearly suggest a wider usage, at least during the nineteenth century.

The embroidered dragon robe we are discussing bears other less familiar motifs. Above the water at the hem, and working from the centre seam outward, are a flaming wheel, a white umbrella, a fish, a canopy, a red knot, a vase, a lotus flower and a shell, all emblems associated with Buddhism. On the main body of the garment back and front, directly beneath the front-facing dragon, is a basket containing peaches and two bamboo flutes. Among the clouds, and not easily recognizable, are a rigid fan, a sword, a bamboo tube with divining rods and a gourd, each repeated four times, with a pair of wooden clappers and a lotus pod appearing twice only. All these motifs, tied about with trailing ribbons, were linked with the group of semi-mythical characters known as the 'Eight Immortals'. These figures had a prominent place in the popular religious and philosophical system known to us as Taoism which was concerned, among other aims, with the search for personal immortality. The cranes flying through the clouds are commonly depicted along with Taoist subjects. The colour of their plumage is the same as that of the white birds supposed to dwell with the Immortals, and their appearance on robes like this serves to reinforce wishes for a long life. The sleeves, the cuffs and the neck binding contain a selection of the so-called 'Eight Precious Objects'. Appearing here are pearls, a circular ornament *(sheng)*, a rectangular ornament *(fang sheng)*, a sceptre, a branch of coral, and rolls of silk often looking more like scroll paintings. [17] The red and white bats scattered over this robe are a visual pun: the Chinese word for bat, pronounced *fu,* sounds the same as and is written with a similar though not identical character to a word for 'happiness'.

We should beware of reading too much into these isolated elements, but taken together they, 'encode a series of personal and social targets common to many individuals in Imperial China – long life, official position, wealth, happiness, and male progeny'. [18] Some Chinese writers have made our task more difficult by their love of grouping mythological figures and their attributes together in such a way as to make us think that each one should never appear outside its group. The 'Eight Buddhist Objects', the 'Eight Taoist Attributes', and the 'Eight Precious Objects' described in connection with this robe were a late codification of motifs which had developed individually over a period of time. There is ample evidence on dress and ceramics in particular that the groups were often not rigidly adhered to. The elements described above will be seen to appear in different combinations on a wide variety of types of garment.

Cut and Origins of the Dragon Robe

Fig. 1 It is apparent from a study of the Museum's untailored garments that three lengths of silk, each the full width of the bolt as it came off the loom, and therefore having selvedges at either side, are needed for the body and upper sleeves. By following the

Opposite: Fig. 1 *Dragon Robe* T.219-1948.

18

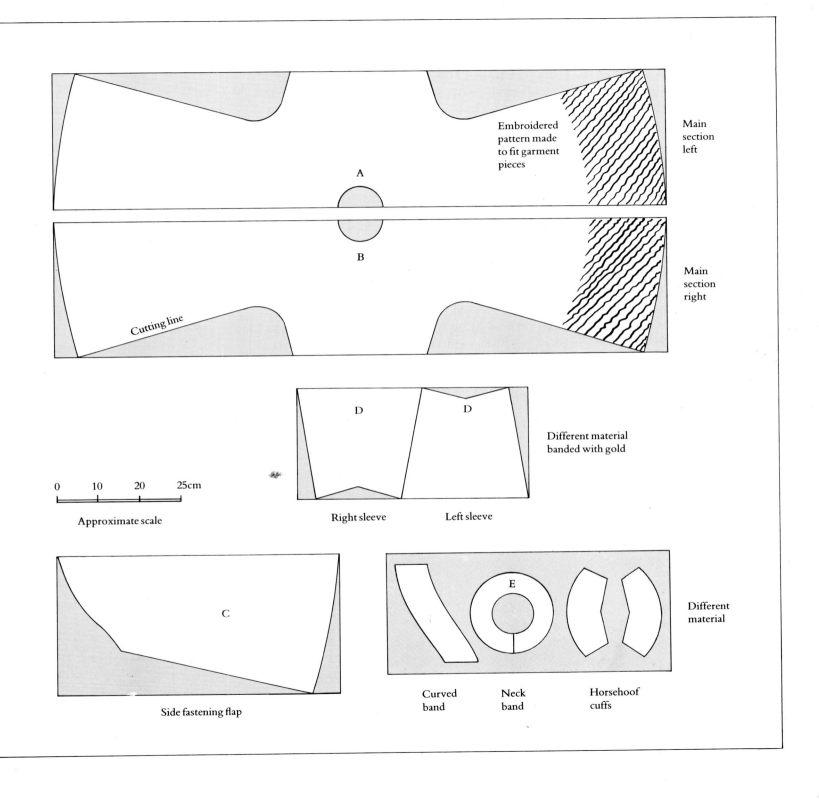

Embroidered pattern made to fit garment pieces

Main section left

A

B

Main section right

Cutting line

D   D

Different material banded with gold

0   10   20   25cm

Approximate scale

Right sleeve   Left sleeve

C

E

Different material

Side fastening flap

Curved band   Neck band   Horsehoof cuffs

line of the decoration on these uncut robes we can see that the left side of the garment, both back and front, and the integral upper sleeve is cut from one of the longer loom widths (A). From the second length of the same size is taken the right side of the back, the other upper sleeve, and the right inside front section (B). There is thus no seam along the shoulders. A straight vertical seam down the centre back joins the two widths together, while the outer side-fastening flap, cut from a third shorter loom width, is joined to the rest of the garment down the centre front selvedge (C). The garment is then folded in half horizontally at shoulder level, and the side seams, narrowing towards the top of the body to give a loosely-shaped silhouette, continue along under the sleeves to join the front to the back. These side edges, unlike the centre seams, will lose their selvedges in the cutting process and are liable to fray. Sometimes the side seams and sometimes all the seams are left unsewn for up to 66cm from the bottom to allow the wearer ease of movement.

All the untailored dragon robe lengths in the Victoria and Albert Museum are embroidered and are already seamed along the central selvedges, a necessary first step prior to embroidering the decoration, as the design must match across the garment. Small holes approximately four centimetres apart along the outside edges of the silk indicate where it was fixed flat and held taut between two beams while the embroidery was being executed. While many dragon robes are embroidered, some have the pattern incorporated as weaving proceeds, so that the garment's shape is revealed on the loom. Apart from some exceptions where the design is woven right across the garment thus obviating the need for central seams, the usual three lengths of material are utilized for woven robes. The most usual technique for these woven robes is that of silk tapestry, in Chinese called *kesi*, 'cut silk', after the
7 vertical slits which occur where one colour ends and the next begins. [19] Tapestry weave is suited to the pictorial patterning of dragon robes because motifs of solid colour are achieved by completely covering the undyed warp (longitudinal) threads with the polychrome weft (horizontal) threads, each colour of which goes back and forth only in its particular pattern area. To achieve the desired effect, there is a certain amount of deliberate distortion of the wefts, and even of the warps, in the hem border decoration. Dragon robes woven this way have selvedges down the centre front and back and at the ends of the upper sleeve, with raw edges at the sides like the embroidered robes, suggesting an underarm section of plain weave in-filling which would have been cut away for tailoring. On both embroidered and woven robes the lower sleeves, always in a contrasting material and usually in plain dark blue, are sometimes banded in gold (D), and terminate in added 'horsehoof cuffs', in Chinese *ma ti xiu,* which together with the curving neckband are cut from another length of material, often different from that used for either the main body or the lower sleeves (E). The cuffs and neckband of silk tapestry robes are woven to shape so they can be smoothly applied without teasing or pleating the material to fit the garment curves.

It has been argued that while the patterning on dragon robes is Chinese, the cut is Manchu. [20] Before an attempt is made to trace this garment shape to its origins the term 'Manchu' should be clarified. The majority population of the empire who

20

called themselves *Han* were ruled from 1644 to 1911 by a people of a different ethnic origin, known in English as the Manchu. Although such a geographical expression is never used in Chinese the members of this ethnic group have given their name in English to Manchuria, the north-eastern region of the present-day People's Republic of China from which they originally came. Their conquest of the preceding Ming dynasty (1368-1644) led to the ascendancy of a Manchu political élite who named their ruling house *Qing*. This ascendancy led also to the imposition of a number of hitherto unknown social habits on the majority Han population. The braiding of mens' hair is the best known example. Mindful of the difference between Manchu and Han Chinese we shall now return to the origins of the garment shape. On opening up the side seams and laying the dragon robe flat it can
Fig. 1 be seen that in making up the garment a certain amount of undecorated silk has been cut away along the sloping edges and there is not enough of this underarm wastage to accommodate the overlapping flap which must, consequently, be cut from another piece of material. The fact that these robes do not use the cloth economically is seen by Dorothy Burnham, an authority on the cut of clothes, as an indication that they may be descended from garments once made from animal skins.[21] Another writer suggests that the forest reindeer hides possibly used for such garments by the ancestors of the Manchus could have provided the armholes for a notional coat which would bear similarities to a sleeveless jacket also seen in the Chinese dress repertory. This theory does not, however, explain the origin of the type of dragon robe with integral upper sleeve under discussion here.[22]

The task of searching out the dragon robe's forebears is made more complex by the scarcity of existing Manchu garments from the period before their conquest of China proper in 1644 but one such robe, of typical dragon robe cut, has been recently published. It is datable to 1632 (not really early enough for our purposes) and is made from Chinese-woven cloud and dragon-patterned silk.[23] Garments of dragon robe shape belonging to peoples who are ethnically related to the Manchus are, it is true, sometimes made from skins. A pair of garments for a Hezhe (formerly called *Gold*) man and woman is made of softened salmon skins pieced together.[24] A Hezhe robe in the Budapest Ethnographic Museum is also made from many skins of small animals but such small individual pieces could not have dictated the final shape of the robe. The side-fastening overlap, rather than following as has been suggested an animal skin's contours, may perhaps follow the line of the human collar bone before it curves down to fasten under the right arm. On a modern skin robe for a woman of the Oroqen, who like the Manchus and Hezhe are a Tungusic-speaking people from north-east China, the curve of the animal's skin has not been utilized for the collar-fastening, but appears at waist-level almost randomly pieced to another section.[25] It seems therefore that if the dragon robe retains a link at all with an earlier skin garment from northern Asia, it is a very tenuous one. We should not assume that clothing cut in such a way as to result in leftover material was originally made, less wastefully, from hides. On the contrary, it may signify a healthy textile industry amply able to fulfil the demands of a prosperous clientele who took fashionable dressing seriously and who were happy to be seen spending their wealth lavishly.

There is a case to be made for the proposition that clothing influences travelled from south to north rather than in the opposite direction as proponents of the skin origin theory would have it. Owen Lattimore, the recognized authority on the Chinese border regions, thinks that the garments of the Hezhe, a people of which he made a close study in the 1920s and 1930s, were in the main Chinese and certainly of Chinese cut. Pertinent to the problem we are concerned with here is his statement that reindeer were not hunted by the Hezhe. [26] An absorbing and detailed analysis of costumes collected by two Danish Central Asian expeditions in the 1930s remarks on the Chinese influence upon Mongolian dress – Mongols and Manchus have historically shared many modes of cultural expression – noting that because cloth was imported from China, the Mongols followed the Chinese way of dressing. [27] In pursuing the argument for a cloth tradition, earlier Chinese garments must be examined for resemblances to Qing clothing as exemplified by dragon robes. Unfortunately, however, few examples of dress from the Ming dynasty survive and there are no whole or unaltered Ming garments in the Victoria and Albert Museum's collection. However, recent excavation reports from China show garments from the mid-thirteenth century through to the early seventeenth century displaying a surprisingly wide variety of styles. A tomb on the outskirts of Fuzhou dated to around 1250, whose occupant would of course have been Han Chinese, contained sixty-four jackets and robes. All have sleeves in prolongation of the body with material added to lengthen them considerably. In all cases the sleeves are wide. Some of the garments are front-opening, and those that fasten at the side appear to have a generous overlapping section joined to the garment along a central seam, identical to those depicted in Ming dynasty portraits and similar to the later dragon robes of the Qing period. The high neck-fastening to the right, however, is not curved as on the Qing garments but the secure and weatherproof closure indicates that we should not assume that such a feature is only appropriate on garments belonging to people living or originating far to the north of Fuzhou, in regions of harsh winters. [28]

From the surviving evidence, admittedly scant, it would appear that garment closures of the type described above had a wider distribution, but it is remarkable that all the robes excavated from the Shandong tomb of a minor official dating from 1350 (when the Mongols ruled China) are markedly different from the side-fastening robes found at Fuzhou despite Shandong's geographical situation in the colder climatic zone of north China. They are cross-over garments, of the type called false front opening, very much like the Japanese *kimono*. [29] The sleeves on clothes from this tomb and from two tombs dated 1603 and 1613 vary considerably both in width and length, showing the existence of numerous different garment types within a single period and undermining the over-simplified opposition between loose 'Ming' garments and tight 'Qing' garments. [30] As far as it is possible to tell, many of these garments have an integral sleeve. This presupposes at least some wastage of silk cut away from under the arms, but none of the varied types of sleeve seem quite so close fitting as those on Qing dragon robes. The pre-Qing

Opposite:
7 *Detail of dragon robe*, silk tapestry weave, late 18th – early 19th century, T.756-1950.

22

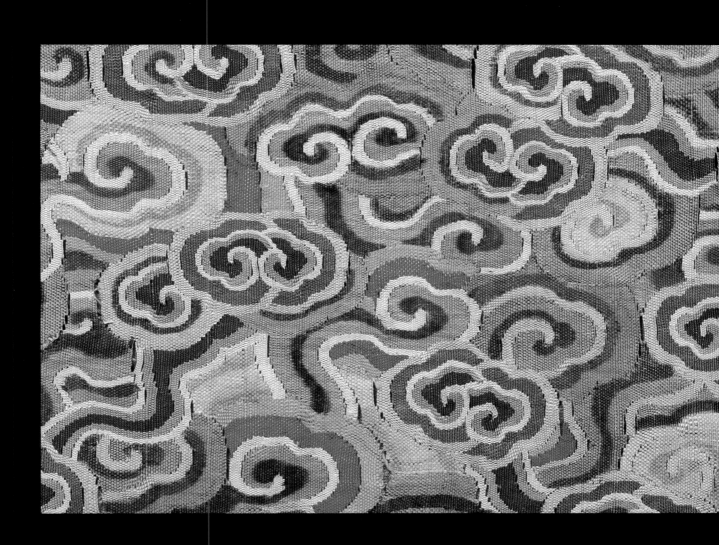

garments so far published seem to lack button fastenings, vertical slits at the hem, and the closer fitting sleeve with protective horsehoof cuff, three characteristics of the Qing dragon robe whose origins we may tentatively assign to the Manchus.

One plausible suggestion put forward to explain the appearance of the dragon robe's contrasting lower sleeve conjectures that pre-conquest Manchus, when altering coveted Ming robes, cut off the wide sleeves at elbow level and added new tighter sleeves in order to avoid making the original sleeves narrower and marring the dragon pattern woven into the silk. [31] However, Ming robes did not always bear identical pattern arrangements and it seems that whatever alteration technique was used, the pattern would inevitably have been spoiled in some way. In any case, although much fuller than Qing robe sleeves, Chinese robes from the Ming period as exemplified by the excavated examples often have sleeves made in three sections. If the sleeve is not an inset one but is cut as an integral part of the body of the garment, there is not sufficient cloth to make it very long. Further cloth must be sewn to it and a contrasting material would be a natural way of adding to a garment's decorative interest. Mongol women's robes, although not bearing dragon robe designs, sometimes had just such a contrasting lower sleeve. [32] A possible conclusion would therefore be that there is no clear rupture between the garment cuts of the Ming and the succeeding Qing periods.

Accessories to the Dragon Robe

In order to arrive at a complete picture of Qing official dress, it is necessary to describe the ensemble of which the dragon robe sometimes formed a part. Portraits surviving from the years before the mid-seventeenth century show Ming officials with large rank badges on the front of their robes. [33] Ye Mengzhu, an author from Shanghai whose memory spanned the late Ming and early Qing dynasties, reminisces for several pages on Ming fashion. He makes the point that the only difference between official Ming costume and that of private wealthy people was the rank badge. We also learn from him that after the Qing conquest, which in the Yangtze valley where he lived took place in 1645, there followed several years of confusion in matters of dress. According to him it was around 1650 that costume rules were promulgated and a new style of dragon-patterned robe with an embroidered 'patch' *(pu)* on front and back became regulation dress *(ming fu)*. He goes on to describe the various birds and animals depicted. [34] Another source confirms the existence of this decree, giving the year more precisely as 1652, and Cammann believes the wearing of the outer coat *(pu fu)* to date from this year. [35]

Out of a collection of some thirty pairs and single squares, Ming badges are not well represented in the Victoria and Albert Museum. Those illustrated can be dated far into Qing times, probably the late eighteenth or early nineteenth centuries. The background is a dark blue satin, a material common to the majority of squares, and the embroidered design is asymmetrical with a scaled and hoofed beast, in Chinese a *qilin,* standing on a rocky promontory and snarling over its shoulder. Floating on

8

24

the waves are a musical stone, a vase containing coral and a sceptre, books and two scrolls. A pine tree clings to the tall rock to the left, while fungus plants and a peony flower grow on the lower rock. The polychrome clouds sail in from the sides of the square, and two bats are unnaturally on the wing in the sunlight. The whole design is framed in a gold key-fret border, and each square is turned under and lined with plain pale blue silk. Under magnification, guide marks for the pattern can be seen in several places as blurred white lines. These lines are very rudimentary, all the details of shading and in-filling being left to the embroiderer's skill. Such imaginative use of colour and stitches is not found on any of the other Qing squares in the Museum, most of which are embroidered. However, less well-executed squares are not without interest for they give us almost the full range of bird and animal motifs.

Those badges that survive in pairs have the design drawn on them in such a way that, when worn, the two identical creatures would face opposite ways. The motif on the majority of squares to be worn on the back would face to the left, while those worn on the front would face to the right. A few reverse this practice and it has been suggested that these may have been for wives of officials. The birds on the respective outer coats would then face each other when an official and his wife were sitting side by side. It is worth pointing out however that in the strictly segregated households of the élite men and women mixed very rarely, celebrating separately even on formal occasions like the New Year. A small number of squares, like the ones reproduced here, show the bird or animal looking over its shoulder away from the general direction of the body. In all cases, however, the creature faces the sun, a design element firmly established by the late seventeenth century.[36]

Many of the nineteenth century squares were deliberately designed to facilitate a change in rank by leaving a central space to be filled successively with the relevant applied animal or bird. On all the Museum's examples these added motifs do not fit the gaps successfully, and the poor quality of the applying stitches make the squares clumsy and unattractive. However, the stitching used to apply the finished squares to the coats is very much neater. Apart from one odd example where European hooks and eyes have been used (T. 163-1969), the rank badges on the Museum's outer coats are turned under and neatly stitched with silk sewing thread. The badge on the front is applied in two sections, one either side of the opening. Several uncut examples show how this was managed without spoiling the central line of the design. One of these (T. 48-1948) has two crane badges embroidered onto a single strip of dark blue satin, one above the other. The top badge, destined for the front, is worked in two halves leaving a vertical strip of undecorated background material through the middle to allow for cutting and turning in. Unused rank badges exist where this allowance has not been made. Unless these show back badges only, we must conclude that they were not made for official outer coats but possibly as souvenirs for foreigners, with whom they were especially popular for making into bags and cushions.[37]

In addition to the round dragon badges (which we shall discuss later in connection with the imperial family) the Museum has an embroidered round crane badge (T.240-1948). This late nineteenth century piece is further evidence of the difficulties of ensuring conformity with strict dress regulations. Its exact function remains a mystery but it may be that the upwardly mobile wearer adopted a round badge as a way of sharing the status of the nobility. Conversely, textual sources also contain illustrations for which no examples are known. The Victoria and Albert Museum's sheets of costume and accessory illustrations, a manuscript (but quite possibly later) edition of the 1759 text *Huang chao li qi tu shi* ('Illustrated Precedents for the Ritual Implements of the Imperial Court'), include several leaves showing garments to be worn by the male dancers who officiated at ritual festivals. [38] The

9 one illustrated, a plain, side-fastened robe, has as its only decoration a square similar in size to the rank badges we have been looking at, but with a mallow flower as the central motif.

We do not know what other garments were worn with this dancer's coat. All the outer coats in the Museum are too short to be the main item of clothing and, having a front-opening with no overlap, they do not fasten very closely across the chest.

10 The seams are left open at each side and at back and front to form slits. One Chinese name for this outer coat, *pu fu*, means 'garment with a patch' but it was also called *wai tao*, meaning 'outer covering', a name which better describes its use. Father Kiong, the author of *Politesse Chinoise*, uses the latter term and describes them as being made from satin or gauze, with sable fur reserved for officials of the third rank and above. A shorter, waist-length surcoat could be substituted for the *wai tao* when travelling or making 'les visites ordinaires'. [39] Those in the Museum's collection are of dark blue satin or plain weave silk, some incorporating a

Below left:
9 *Design for a coat to be worn by a male dancer,* watercolour on silk, 42.5 × 41 cm, D.226-1904.

Below right:
10 *Man's outer coat with embroidered rank badge,* dark blue plain weave silk with satin weave roundels, wadded, late 19th century, 113 × 168 cm, T.104-1958.

self-patterned roundel design. The one illustrated, dating from the nineteenth century, is padded, the wadding material being held in place by regular straight quilting stitches through both top and lining. Each coat is cut from two lengths of silk which are seamed together down the centre back and left open at the front. Extra pieces of silk are used to make the sleeves longer, and inserted triangular segments increase the width of the hem. For a much earlier period Ye Mengzhu has this to say about the length of the surcoat:

> 'From the 24th or 25th years of the Kangxi reign (1685/1686) robes in the capital gradually became shorter while the *wai tao* gradually became longer. In the old days a short *wai tao* came to the waistline, while a long one was one which came to the knees. Now they are never more than five inches *(cun)* shorter than the robe'.[40]

The Museum's examples, which date from the nineteenth century, vary in length from 113cm to 132cm from neck to hem.

Both Father Kiong and Ye Mengzhu write at some length about official hats, and these may well have been more important in distinguishing rank than other items of dress. Such hats had fringes of red silk cords or dyed yak's hair covering the crowns which were topped with a spherical knob of variously coloured glass, semi-precious stone or metal according to the wearer's status. Summer hats were conical in shape and woven from various types of split cane and straw. Ye Mengzhu tells us that when these cane hats were first introduced in 1646 'there were none in the shops in south China, and they had to be cut out of baskets and mats'.[41] For the period spanning the late nineteenth and early twentieth centuries – and it is from this time that the Museum's examples date – Shandong province supplied nearly the whole empire with straw summer hats. The British Consul-General Hosie distinguishes between those made of straw and a more elaborate type for high officials made of split bamboo. These were made on an hereditary cottage industry basis in the villages around Chengdu in Sichuan, the vast southwestern province of which Hosie made a meticulous survey. The bamboo framework was covered inside and out with coloured silk gauze, and over this was a fine transparent netting woven from bamboo fibre. These better quality hats took two days or more to weave. [42] One of the summer hats in the Museum conforms closely to this type except that it does not have an outer netting of bamboo fibre. The framework is here only covered with white silk gauze. The displacement of certain warp (longitudinal) elements from their parallel position, which gives gauze weave its singular character, here occurs after every fifth passing of the weft. A striped effect is thus achieved, with the openwork gauze weave line recurring between the more solid sections of plain weave. To cover the hat the gauze is turned sideways from the direction in which it was woven so that the stripes are vertical. In common with other hats of this type this example is edged with a black and gold silk binding, and has a pearl-like bead attached to the centre front. There is a stiffened circle inside, and ties for securing it to the head.

Winter hats were different in shape, having a crown of dark blue satin and an upturned brim often trimmed with fur. The winter hat shown in an early

11 *Summer hat*, bamboo, white gauze weave silk, red silk cord fringe, late 19th century, 21 cm, T.214-1934.

12 *Detail of summer hat* showing gauze weave's characteristic crossed warps between blocks of plain weave, T.214-1934.

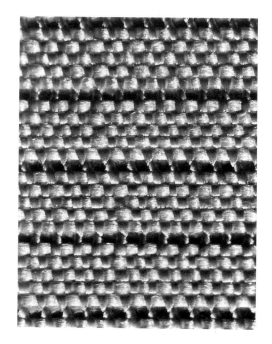

13 nineteenth century watercolour has a peacock feather decoration sloping down over the neck. These plumes were awarded to officers for meritorious services. An example in the Museum (T.147-1959) with its extant shop label from the Wan Sheng Yong Feather Shop in the main shopping street of Peking shows how readily available these insignia of honour were at least in the nineteenth and twentieth
14 centuries. The one winter hat in the collection has a black velvet brim and its own silk plait attached at the back. All men in China, whether they were officials or not, were required to shave the front of their heads and wear this braided style during the Qing dynasty (1644-1911). Although many men achieved sufficient length of hair for this purpose, supplementary hair could be purchased.

It has been thought that a wide detachable collar was closely associated with court dress. Photographs and watercolours make it clear that this accessory was frequently worn as part of the full costume of civil servants and not exclusively reserved for use with the dragon-patterned but differently-cut court robes. A group of clothes and accessories which came into the Museum as a matching set of dragon robe garments includes such a collar while a late nineteenth century line drawing of

13 *Official*, watercolour on paper, c.1800-1810, from a volume 40.6 × 31.7 cm, 8965.

14 *Winter hat, collar and boots*, from a set of dragon robe insignia for a Ninth Rank Official, late 19th century, T.40-1956.

a collar of the same type shows it to be an accepted accessory of the standard dragon robe and outer coat which are featured alongside it on the same page. [43]

Cammann finds first mention of this collar in an eighteenth century administrative compendium, under an entry for 1625, where it is called a *pi ling*, a 'shoulder collar'. [44] John Vollmer speculates on its possible ancestry, believing the shape to resemble an opened-out hood. [45] However, the fact that it is stiffened and shaped so that the points spread out beyond the body make it fit into that class of garments, found in many cultures, which are designed to emphasize men's shoulders. The *pi ling* whether embroidered or woven with dragon designs against a dark blue ground was generally bordered with a wide band of blue and gold silk. It was either attached to the top button of the outer coat by means of loops, or else had its own independent closing device.

5   In the photograph shown in Plate 5 the Chinese military official is wearing a much smaller unadorned collar *(ling tou)* which, in the absence of a *pi ling,* perhaps served to neaten what might otherwise have been an untidy neckline. His insignia are completed by a long loop of beads, having four shorter straight strings attached
15 to it, three falling to the front and one down the back. Surviving necklaces in this style are made from various precious and semi-precious stones, glass, coral and enamelled metal. The black satin boots on high white soles were the customary footwear with this ensemble and could be very expensive. Their purchase price in 1865 was roughly equivalent to a servant's wages for a year. [46]

Men's Dress at Court

Fashion, comfort, and the weather must all normally have been taken into account when the emperor decided what to wear. However, there is one type of garment worn by the emperor about which we can be more specific as to at least some of the
16 occasions on which it was worn. This is the distinctive full-skirted garment, different from the dragon robe in several respects despite having dragon ornamentation, called in Chinese *chao fu,* 'court robe' or 'audience robe'. It was used by other people at court besides the emperor and as we shall see women's differed
17 from men's. The translation 'audience robe' provides a clue that in some cases it was worn in the presence of royalty. This is confirmed in the novel *The Story of the Stone,* completed c. 1760, where the women of the Jia family who hold hereditary titles dress in *chao fu* to make the formal New Year visit to the palace where one of the Jia daughters is an imperial concubine. [47] A Chinese textile historian writing about a yellow court robe which belonged to the Qianlong emperor (r. 1736-1795) tells us that such robes were worn by the emperor on the occasions of the palace examinations, imperial weddings, the winter solstice, the Sacrifices to Heaven and Earth, and other such ritual and sacrificial occasions. [48] This garment in gauze weave silk for summer wear includes twelve symbols in the pattern arrangement as
18 does the robe in the Victoria and Albert Museum illustrated here. These twelve
19 symbols have been viewed quite correctly in many instances as insignia of the

15 *Necklace* from a set of dragon robe insignia, yellow, pink and green glass, late 19th century, T.40-1956.

29

reigning emperor and his immediate family.

Although these twelve motifs undoubtedly have ancient roots, visual evidence for these roots is now mostly lacking. Imperial portraits from the Ming dynasty show emperors wearing what appear to be twelve symbol garments, although only ten at most of the emblems are in fact visible. [49] As to their meaning, we cannot now explain them individually. The importance attached to them and their antiquity has produced reinterpretations in Chinese texts over the centuries. In trying to clarify these texts, and so come to a greater understanding of each motif's meaning, we are in danger of achieving the very opposite. The important point about these twelve symbols is surely their elusive numinous quality. The Museum's golden yellow
16 court robe is decorated with a sun and moon embroidered on the left and right shoulders respectively and a star constellation above the head of the front dragon, with a symmetrical linear motif to the left of it and an axe head to the right. Grains of millet in a circle and a square of flames are included in the decorated skirt band. Not visible in the reproduction are a mountain, a pair of small dragons and a bird on the upper part, with cups and waterweed on the skirt.

It is strange that these imperial motifs are so small and in no way dominate the decorative scheme. They seem almost insignificant by contrast with the major elements of the pattern. Although we cannot be sure when the Qing emperors started using them, the first Qing reference to these twelve symbols is in the

16 *Man's twelve symbol court robe*, embroidery on yellow twill weave silk, late 19th century, 146 × 218 cm, T.753-1950.

17 *Portrait of a Provincial Treasurer, Lu Ming*, watercolour on silk, 18th century, 215.5 × 103 cm, E.360-1956.

Opposite:
8 *Pair of rank badges*, embroidery on satin weave silk, late 18th – early 19th century, 27 × 27 cm, T.164-1965.

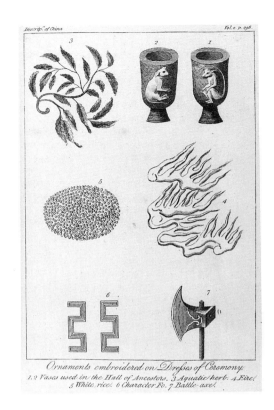

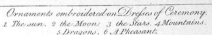

Ornaments embroidered on Dresses of Ceremony.
1 The sun. 2 the Moon. 3 the Stars. 4 Mountains.
5 Dragons. 6 A Pheasant.

Ornaments embroidered on Dresses of Ceremony.
1.2 Vases used in the Hall of Ancestors. 3 Aquatic herb. 4 Fire.
5 White rice. 6 Character Fo. 7 Battle-axe.

Illustrated Precedents for the Ritual Utensils of the Imperial Court of 1759, by which date the familiar dragon, cloud and water decoration was well established. None of the Chinese written texts specify where the symbols should be positioned on the robe. However the court robes in the *Illustrated Precedents* show, on one type, all the symbols confined to the top part of the robe. On another type which more closely resembles the Museum's example the symbols are placed as described above but with two exceptions. The cups and waterweed are on the back of the actual robe, whereas in the graphic source they are on the front. The latter seems to be the usual arrangement on other surviving examples. The Museum's robe shows no obvious sign of alteration, suggesting that the skirt pieces may inadvertently have been wrongly tailored in the first place. Its consequent unacceptability for court use may be the reason why it became available for ultimate acquisition by the Museum. Few twelve symbol court robes survive outside China.

The other court robes in the collection do not bear twelve symbols. In the Museum records they are all described as 'blue'. However, on closely examining these robes, while the warp (longitudinal) threads can certainly be called blue, the weft (horizontal) threads are seen to be grey or pale green. Both sets of yarn were probably dyed with indigo prior to weaving. Those destined for the warp had the natural gum washed out of them allowing the dye to be readily absorbed and resulting in a rich blue colour. The weft threads, however, were not degummed or only partially so and as a consequence the dye penetrated less well and a more muted colour was obtained. In the case of the plain and twill weave court robes, the warp threads even when combined in pairs are finer than the weft threads. The latter therefore predominate, giving the finished textile a pronounced green or grey tinge. This tinge is less obvious on the gauze weave robes because of the open nature of the weave, but on these too the weft is not a true blue whereas the warp is. The court robes of silk tapestry in the Victoria and Albert Museum are of poor quality. It is therefore difficult to tell if the blue wefts have been beaten over the natural coloured warps in a deliberately loose way in order to make the resulting background colour a less dense blue. We should note in this connection that while modern Chinese writers use the word *lan* meaning 'blue' to describe these robes, Qing writers refer to them as *shi qing,* 'slate grey'. [50] Although brown court robes exist in western collections the most commonly encountered colour is the blue described above. Most of the emperor's court robes appear to have been yellow but he did wear blue when sacrificing to the God of Grain and when praying for rain, red at the spring equinox when praying at the Altar of the Sun, and a *yue bai* 'moon white' garment at the autumn equinox when praying at the Altar of the Moon. A colour plate of a *yue bai* court robe in Peking shows it to be turquoise. A red court robe pictured in the same source lacks the twelve symbols and is captioned as having belonged to the Yongzheng emperor (r. 1723-1735). [51]

Cut and Origins of the Court Robe

Schuyler Cammann believes that the complicated tailoring of court robes is due to their makeshift origin. He assumes that like the dragon robes they evolved from cut-down Ming robes, and that in early Qing they consisted of two separate
20 sections. [52] A skirt in the Victoria and Albert Museum, similar in cut and design to the lower part of a court robe, is the only piece of evidence ever cited for the existence of this notional former two-piece court robe. [53] It is certainly true that the style of embroidery would date this satin skirt to the relatively early period of the eighteenth century but as there is now no way of telling whether it was originally joined to an upper section or not it may always have been a separate garment. The matching jacket is not in the collection and has always been presumed missing, but it is just as likely that it never existed. Skirts such as these could have been worn over the top of other robes, provided there was an outer coat to conceal the waist-line.
21 Portraits show that it was not unknown for outer coats to be used with court robes. Worn in this possibly cost-cutting way however, the design style and bindings of the protruding horsehoof cuffs of the robe beneath would, strictly speaking, have had to match the separate court skirt. This lack of matching may not have mattered in the nineteenth century when dress etiquette seems to have been more lax but marked differences between cuffs and skirt would probably not have been acceptable in the eighteenth century. So while there are poor quality court skirts likely to have been used in this way in existence, the Victoria and Albert Museum's

Opposite:
18 *Ornaments embroidered on Dresses of*
19 *Ceremony* from Abbé Grosier, *A General Description of China,* (London 1788).

Above:
20 *Court skirt,* embroidery on dark blue satin weave silk, early 18th century, 91 cm, T.251-1966.

33

example remains unique at the time of writing both for its superb needlework and for the as yet unsolved problems it poses about the origin of the cut.

None of the Chinese written sources studied so far mention the possibility of an original two-piece court robe and recent archaeological work has produced positive evidence against this hypothesis. A one-piece robe with full, pleated skirt and a lobed dragon pattern on the shoulders, chest and back belonging to a Ming prince was found in Shandong province and is datable to the late fourteenth century. This robe is called a *long pao* 'dragon robe' in the excavation report on the prince's tomb and is described as darkish yellow, 'the colour of corn'. [54] Another robe of similar cut was excavated from a tomb outside Nanjing and belonged to a Ming dynasty dignitary who lived from 1450 to 1517. [55] Dress nomenclature of the Ming dynasty differed from that of the Qing, as did the garments themselves and the occasions on which they were worn. However these one-piece full-skirted robes, one with imperial connections and the other with high-ranking military connections, provide us with convincing evidence of a pattern on which the later, one-piece Qing court robe was almost certainly based.

The nineteenth century yellow court robe in the Museum's collection is woven in a twill weave silk. Unlike plain weave, in which one weft goes over one warp and under the next, twill weave is characterized by oblique lines formed on the cloth. In this example, the weft goes under two warps and over one, and on each successive line of weaving the points of intersection move outward and upward by one warp, producing the diagonals. On this robe the twill direction is to the right causing the lines to show up less distinctly than they might because the direction of the twist in the warp threads is also to the right. On some of the other court robes the twilling is more prominent because the diagonals in the weave go in the opposite direction from the twist in the yarn. The weft threads have no appreciable twist to them, and both warps and wefts are dyed the same shade of yellow.

The robe, in common with the Museum's blue examples, consists of four main parts. The top, cut in a similar way to the dragon robe, with an overlapping front section and no shoulder seams, has the familiar lower sleeves attached to it above elbow level. These paler yellow lower sleeves, terminating in blue horsehoof cuffs, are banded with gold-wrapped threads which are laid onto the silk and secured, or 'couched down', in pairs with orange silk. The skirt is gathered into a separate waistband which is decorated with two elongated dragons facing each other. This, in turn, is sewn to the upper part of the robe, the joins being covered with decorative blue and gold binding with a scrolling flower design, and more couched gold. Two overlapping sections make up the skirt. The top of the skirt has been tucked with even box pleats which are called *bi ji*, 'piled-up pleats'. They are not as close together as those on the blue skirt but the careful pleat construction is otherwise unsurpassed among the Museum's other court robes, several of which are merely skimpily gathered with no pleating at all. The quality of the embroidery is good and the standard colour scheme of shaded reds, greens, blues, yellows, and white includes the bright mauve used in the second half of the nineteenth century (p. 118). There is silver-coloured couching as well as gold on the large dragons. In

Opposite:
21 *Portrait of a general, Lu Jiangui*, watercolour on silk, 18th century, 211 × 99 cm, E.362-1956.

Above:
22 *Robe of Prince Zhu Tan*, excavated from his tomb in Shandong province, late 14th century, 130 cm.

35

the curve of the front facing dragon's body at the top of the garment is a stylized and symmetrical Chinese character, *shou*, 'long life'. This design motif replaces the usual pearl on some, though by no means all, twelve symbol garments of both dragon and court robe cut.

17   An eighteenth century painting of Lu Ming, a Chinese provincial treasurer, shows his court robe worn without any outer garment. This is also the style most often seen in imperial portraits. [56] Court robes were worn with the wide collar discussed earlier and, like dragon robes, were tightly belted. Draw-string purses suspended from the belt by silk cords served as pockets. The small square of bordered material attached at waist-level on the right hand side of the court robes illustrated here is not a pocket and in most cases serves no practical purpose. It may perhaps represent a vestigial scabbard-slide, designed to hold a sword in place across the body. Its Chinese name is *ren*, a term used only to refer to this curious appendage. On some robes it is attached beyond the main skirt while on others it falls over the top of the skirt. Robes in the former style sometimes have loop fastenings attached to the reverse side of the *ren* and these close over buttons sewn onto the back skirt section.

The Museum's twelve symbol court robe is lined throughout with yellow silk and was designed for spring and autumn wear. Other styles used during these two seasons were embroidery on satin or a self-patterned silk, and silk tapestry. Some of them may have been padded with cotton or silk wadding and for winter they were edged and lined with fur. Silk tapestry was also considered suitable for summer, as was embroidered gauze weave silk. [57]

While we can assign court robes in collections outside China to certain seasons and occasions, we will never be able to establish their imperial ownership. In the absence of any accurate record, it is meaningless to take the few subjective accounts of emperors' heights as evidence when trying to assign certain robes to certain reigns. In any case, what was fashionable as regards length in one year was not so in the next (p. 27).

Other Dress Styles Worn by the Emperor

In our discussions of dragon robes we mentioned that this style of dress was sometimes adopted by the emperor. Several dragon robes with blue and yellow grounds in the Museum's collection carry twelve symbols. We cannot know whether these particular robes were ever worn by any of the ten successive emperors of Qing China or, if they were, by which ones. According to a contemporary Chinese writer, there are today about ten thousand robes stored in the Palace Museum in Peking. [58] Even if we assume that many of these are not twelve symbol garments it seems reasonable to guess that more of them were made than were actually used. Perhaps some never found their way into the palace precincts at all, particularly during the nineteenth century from which most of the garments in the Victoria and Albert Museum date. The loosening of imperial control over the manufacture of these textiles may have led to their circulation among a wider community.

Apart from certain ritual aspects of his life, which were strictly bound by code, we do not know what prompted an emperor's choice of clothes. We cannot be precise about what he wore, and in what combinations. Over his dragon robe he 23 may have worn an outer coat with four round dragon medallions in place of two square rank badges. Hereditary nobles and close relatives of the emperor also wore this kind of coat. From the examples in the Museum we cannot tell with certainty what distinguishes the outer coat of an emperor from those of his nobles. One of these dragon medallion coats, however, incorporates four of the twelve symbols (T.754-1950) and can perhaps lay claim to being for imperial wear, in which case it should be called a *gun fu,* a 'royal robe'. A portrait miniature dated to 1753 depicting 24 the Qianlong emperor (r.1736-1796) shows him wearing an elegant plum-coloured robe unadorned except for a subdued roundel pattern woven into the fabric. This was the kind of apparel most often worn by gentlemen of wealth. As we have seen, more sumptuous garments played their part in the ceremonial aspects of the emperor's life and in choosing such a plain garment the emperor emphasized the more refined and abstemious aspects of his rule. A garment of this simpler type in

23 *Nobleman's outer coat with embroidered dragon roundels*, dark blue twill weave silk, early 19th century, 115 × 160 cm, 05628 I.S.

On the following pages:
24 *Portrait miniature of the Qianlong emperor,* from a presentation book, watercolour on paper, 1753, 22 × 12 cm, L.3285-1975.

25 *Man's robe*, satin weave silk with twill weave roundels, late 18th – early 19th century, 133 × 214 cm, T.128-1966.

古韻

文長　　快臣　　莞田　　蘇意　　趙期印　臨

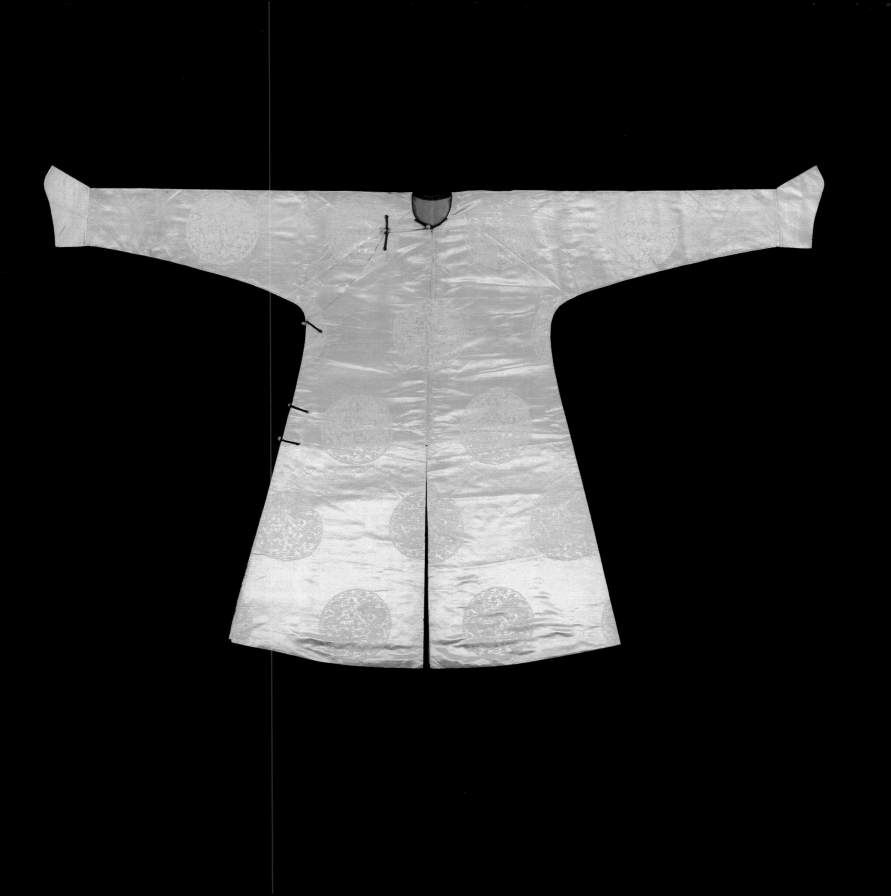

25 the collection is cut from yellow silk with twill weave roundels woven across a satin ground and has no contrasting material in its make-up, extra sections of the plain satin being used for the lower sleeves and horseshoe cuffs. It is particularly soft and supple to the touch, and the pronounced sheen on the satin sets off the dragon roundels well. The design has been matched across the seams and the side fastening. This garment, which has no association with any of the emperors of China, simply represents a mode of dress popular amongst the ruling class of which the emperor was the most exalted member. Some of the robes believed to have belonged to emperors have yellow as a background colour, but it is a golden yellow with less of a green tone than the yellow roundel robe illustrated. As we have seen, the emperor did not always wear yellow and even golden yellow was not exclusively reserved for his use. A painting in Peking depicting entertainments for the Qianlong emperor shows many officers of the imperial guard but noticeably not the emperor wearing this particular shade of 'imperial' yellow. [59] Empresses also seem to have had garments of this colour.

Women's Dress at Court

Although for the most part noblewomen led separate lives from noblemen, they too would wear formal robes as the occasion demanded. We have seen how the women of the Jia family donned court robes to pay a visit to court. It was the empress who officiated at the annual sacrifice to the patroness of silk and it is likely she wore a court robe at such a ceremony.

26 Unless some of the robes now designated male attire were originally also used by women, the Museum has only one identifiable woman's court robe. It is of yellow satin, richer in colour than the male garment studied above, and immaculately embroidered with typical dragon robe designs. Unlike a standard dragon robe, however, all the ribbon clouds embroidered onto the sleeves are turned on end, and the binding round the armholes is found to conceal a seam in the yellow silk. The sleeves on this robe are thus inset and not cut all in one with the garment body. A robe of this shape can perhaps seriously claim to be the final form of what may originally have been two garments. As we shall see, a front-fastening coat without sleeves was generally worn over a woman's court robe in the eighteenth and nineteenth centuries, perhaps indicating such an origin. Binding of a different pattern to that concealing the armhole seam is sewn around the skirt and hem. Its use here is another distinguishing feature of women's court robes. This material, especially woven to be used as such, is dark blue and patterned in gold with small dragon roundels and auspicious emblems. It is identical to that found on the eighteenth century court skirt as well as some of the other court robes in the collection. The same binding can be seen at the horsehoof-shaped ends of the sleeves and, further up the sleeve, it is used to outline an extra sleeveband embroidered in a similar way to the cuffs. This extra band never appears on men's robes; it is found on some but not all women's garments.

Portraits of women from the ruling house show them wearing yellow robes similar to the Museum's female court robe. [60] Like the Museum's own portrait of the wife of Lu Ming they all show the court robe beneath a long sleeveless coat and despite

27 this concealment we can see that the court robe hem is depicted in each case edged with similar blue and gold binding to that on surviving garment examples. At shoulder level, the distinctive armhole edging is much more exaggerated in the portraits than on the Museum's court robe. Similarly, the robes and the paintings show two distinctively different wave patterns at the hem. The extra sleevebands are not at all clearly shown on the blue robe worn by Lu Ming's wife, although on

28 that worn by another Mrs Lu, General Lu Jiangui's wife, there is some attempt at depicting a different band above the tucked plain lower sleeve. This is also a blue court robe, and one of an unfamiliar type. These two portraits, both executed in the mid-eighteenth century, provide evidence for varying styles of women's court robes, most of which no longer exist. The different accessories and the way they may have been worn are also well shown.

The Museum has three examples of sleeveless overgarments which were

29 probably worn with women's court robes. The one illustrated is rendered very heavy by the numerous brass studs on the velvet trim and by the intricate tasselled fringe without which the coat would not be full-length. Neither of these decorative

26 *Woman's court robe*, embroidery on yellow satin weave silk, early 19th century, 138.5 × 168 cm, T.43-1952.

28 *Portrait of Lu Jiangui's wife*, watercolour on silk, 18th century, 211 × 99 cm, E.363-1956.

On the following pages:

27 *Portrait of Lu Ming's wife*, watercolour on silk, 18th century, 215.5 × 103 cm, E.361-1956.

29 *Woman's overgarment*, satin weave silk ground with dragon design formed by both supplementary pattern wefts and brocading wefts, late 18th – early 19th century, 140 cm, T.14-1957.

41

30 *Detail of woman's yellow dragon robe,*
    showing the beaded dark blue cuff section.
    late 19th century, T.253-1967.

31 *Woman's dragon robe,* yellow plain weave
    silk with tapestry weave roundels and
    trimmings, 19th century, 172 × 190 cm,
    T.766-1950.

features are found in portraits of women wearing court dress. Another example is identical to this except that the predominant colour is white (T.193-1948). The third example, of blue silk tapestry (T.871-1901) has no tassels and is bound with the same blue and gold silk found on many court robes. The dragons do not dominate the design as they do on the yellow and white coats, and the clouds are more closely packed together. There is a wave pattern hem with flowers woven among the stripes. In the two portraits the protruding epaulette-like additions look as if they could be part of the outer sleeveless coat rather than the court robe worn beneath it, but no such garment has as yet come to light.

27
28

The empress and other female members of the imperial family, perhaps uniquely for women, also wore standard dragon robes. The Museum has two twelve symbol robes, both yellow and both with extra bands around the sleeves. One of these although having a cramped design and a graceless mountain motif across the central seam is nevertheless very skilfully embroidered with small pearls and coral beads. Other dragon robes in the collection which may have been connected with the ladies of the Manchu court form a group bearing four or six of the twelve symbols, with yellow or light orange as their background colour. All have extra sleevebands. There is also a dragon robe variant without the hem border decoration and with the nine golden dragons confined to roundels. The fur-edged horsehoof cuffs on this garment were designed to be worn turned back and the garment is lined throughout with fur. Its design arrangement, and the fact that it is yellow, make it one of the few extant examples to accord closely with the *Illustrated Precedents* of 1759. [61] Although this states that this type of dragon robe was worn only by empresses and dowager empresses we have no proof that the rules were carried out in practice and we cannot therefore unquestioningly assign the Museum's robe to such exalted owners.

30

31

We do not know whether women members of the imperial family wore long-sleeved outer coats over their dragon robes as the men sometimes did. There are far fewer pictorial representations of women, and those portraits we have already mentioned show them in court robes. A photograph of the Dowager Empress Cixi taken in about 1900 shows her wearing a dragon robe without a coat over the top. [62] For a much earlier period, in a magnificent painting (dated in accordance with 1736) in the Cleveland Museum of Art entitled 'In My Heart is the Power to Reign Peaceably' neither the empress nor any of the Qianlong emperor's concubines are wearing outer garments over their roundel-style dragon robes. [63]

Dragon robes and court robes would not have been the only form of attire for women of the court. Like the emperor, they would have worn the appropriate fashionable dress of the day similar to some of the Manchu women's robes we shall be discussing. Early twentieth century photographs of the Dowager Empress Cixi show her in more sumptuous versions of these. [64] She obviously enjoyed clothes and paid careful attention to her appearance. Some of the robes she wears in these photographs appear identical to examples still in existence in western collections. However, rather than assume that they therefore must have belonged to her, we should perhaps consider them as copies bought by ladies who were keen to emulate a fashion set by the Dowager Empress. With the exception of the Dowager Empress Cixi, who was photographed, and whose lifetime spanned the gradual opening up of court life, no previous rulers would have been in a position to initiate major fashion trends. People who lived away from the capital and who were rich enough to consider clothes as something more than practical body covering would not necessarily have looked to the Manchu court in Peking for guidance on the latest styles, especially if they were Han Chinese.

We should note too that the degree of interest each emperor took in dress must have varied considerably although, with one exception, evidence for this has yet to be published. The Kangxi emperor (r. 1662–1722), in a uniquely informal set of personal letters written to one of his eunuchs in 1697, mentions clothes frequently and is quite specific about styles. Travelling away from the capital he writes:

'Some time ago the silk store had two fur coats, one wolf and one desert fox, though they had not been faced. Have these two coats finished, using *Yü* satin for the sleeves and *Ling-ning* silk for the bodies; when they are done, send them along with one of the batches of memorials. They mustn't be made too tight. Because the lot you sent along with the memorials last time were too tight, they were really uncomfortable. You must be careful.' [65]

Other Dress Styles

Women's Dress

Our study of court dress revealed some of the distinctions between female and male attire. Women of Manchu origin dressed differently from women of the Han Chinese majority although each style borrowed from the other and it is not always possible to distinguish between the two when looking at the Museum's collection of Qing dress. Speaking generally, however, we can say that Manchu women wore full-length gowns while Han Chinese women wore skirts beneath shorter robes with wider sleeves.

Bearing in mind the division (albeit blurred) between Manchu and Han Chinese styles let us look first at the dragon robe adaptations worn by women of the two nationalities. Women did not themselves hold office, but sometimes alluded to their husbands' rank by wearing freer and more inventive versions of the dragon robe insignia. We have no information as to when they wore this kind of clothing, for their circumscribed way of life meant they had no public duties outside the home. Perhaps because they were far less often seen in public than men, women felt able to interpret dress traditions in a freer way. From the detailed descriptions of clothes in the eighteenth century novel *The Story of the Stone* it seems that dress may have been one of the very few areas of real choice and expression open to women. [66] Ye Mengzhu confirms this licence in women's official dress and for the nineteenth century we find evidence in surviving examples. [67]

Apart from those dragon robes which bear some of the twelve symbols in their design, the Museum has very few standard dragon robes with the extra sleevebands thought to have been favoured by Manchu women.

While some male-designated dragon robes and outer coats may have belonged to Manchu women, it seems they preferred to wear different robes from men. Two late nineteenth century examples illustrated here bear this out. Both robes retain the shaped cuffs but they are ostentatiously enlarged. On the turquoise green robe the wave pattern hem is decorated with flowers and bats, which are repeated in the roundels and scattered motifs embroidered above it. The red gown's decoration appears ordered and confined by comparison and although dragons based on archaic designs flank the gold 'long life' character at the centre of each roundel, the more familiar nine scaled dragons are missing. Another coat has two outward-facing dragons at the top of the garment on either side of the front opening. This robe can plausibly be dated to the first half of the eighteenth century. As it seems likely always to have been front fastening it was presumably meant to be worn over another garment, possibly one with horsehoof-shaped cuffs which would have extended beyond the straight sleeves. Although we cannot be entirely certain, several early Qing pictorial sources make it likely that this vigorously patterned piece of weaving of unusual style and quality was intended to be worn by a woman. [68]

35   A Han Chinese woman's robe is shown in a nineteenth century portrait of the wife of an official. It is red and dragon-patterned and has extremely wide, loose sleeves. Beneath it is a panelled skirt and on top is a sleeveless overgarment, both also dragon-patterned, the latter having a rank badge applied to the front. Garments of all these three types as well as the scalloped collar are represented in the Museum and show the general style worn by Han Chinese women on the most formal occasions. Several wide-sleeved robes in the collection have the rank badge embroidered straight onto the garment's background silk.

   We will now look at the far larger number of women's robes which do not bear 36 dragon designs. The dark blue velvet robe in plate 36 has the large sleeves often thought to be a survival from the Ming dynasty (1368-1644). However, women from that dynasty would not have seen many similarities between their clothes and this Qing garment if we are to judge from the paintings and the few extant examples of women's dress which survive from the Ming period. [69] The dangers of over-simplification where garment types are concerned, already revealed by the recent archaeological evidence cited above are confirmed by one writer who refers to distinct northern and southern styles of Ming costume, the difference between them being retained throughout the seventeenth and eighteenth centuries. [70] By this time there was also a Manchu influence at work. The northern style was more conservative than that from the south which was itself very varied and underwent constant innovations because it developed around the commercial silk-producing cities of the lower Yangtze region. The ladies in *The Story of the Stone* apparently dressed in the more modish southern style and it was through women like them that the fashion of the day, in cheaper and less lavish versions, filtered through to families of more modest means. Ye Mengzhu confirms this for the end of the seventeenth century when he writes:

> 'Fashions begin in the homes of the gentry, and are copied by their maids and concubines, who transmit them in their leisure time to their immediate relatives and thus to the villages'. [71]

After 1800 the dividing line between all the different styles became progressively less clear, but the velvet robe can be classified as a typical example of the Han Chinese style even though it dates from the second half of the nineteenth century. The general shape of this robe with central seams, and sleeves cut all in one with the body will be familiar by now. The selvedges are not visible, as the garment is securely lined throughout with red silk. A technical study carried out at the Royal Ontario Museum revealed that a group of Chinese velvets of different dates all have distinctive tubular selvedges. The Chinese suggest that velvet weaving goes back to the second century B.C. and cite the recent find of looped-warp fabrics at Mawangdui near Changsha in south China as evidence. Another theory suggests that velvet weaving was introduced from Europe. European literary sources show that it was in demand in the Far East during the sixteenth century and that it was being produced in China itself by 1592. Seventeenth century Chinese velvets share

35 *Portrait of a Han Chinese woman, watercolour on silk, 19th century, 182.5 × 112 cm, E.606-1954.*

37 *Uncut edgings for a woman's robe, embroidery on white satin weave silk, late 19th – early 20th century, Circ. 305-1930.*

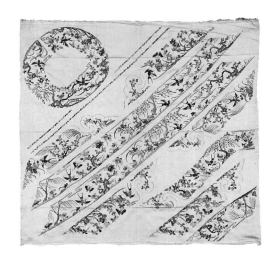

certain technical features with Spanish velvets, pointing to Spain as the possible source. [72] This warp-pile velvet, commonly called simply velvet and utilizing a different weave technique from the early looped-warp fabrics, is made by introducing rods into extra warps above a ground weave. When a section of weaving is complete, the rods can either be slipped out leaving the resulting pile as loops or else these loops can be cut so forming densely-packed tufts imparting a lustrous soft quality to the fabric. In the example shown here, the pattern is in cut velvet against an uncut ground. A simple uncut velvet was woven first and, with the rods left in, the design of flowers and butterflies was transferred to the pile which was then only cut along the pattern lines.

The width of each piece of velvet, at least 51 cm, accommodates the generous sleeves without the addition of extra material, although in common with other ladies' robes of the nineteenth century this one has contrasting embroidered cuffs. The decoration of these would be visible when the hands were held in front of the body in the customary polite and demure posture. The shaped collar is here sewn down onto the garment although many similar collars are detachable. Black satin embroidered with flowers and fantastic birds is used along the line of closure, the 37 side seams and the hem. Uncut examples of similar edgings show how these were made. The shapes were marked onto the silk so that their outlines ran at an acute angle to the warp. When the bands had been filled with embroidery they were cut out, the bias direction facilitating their smooth application to the edges of the garment. Woven ribbons as well as the wider embroidered edgings were additionally applied as trimmings on robes of this kind. Here there is a very narrow, predominantly white, trim around the curling shapes of the collar and side seams, and a different trim along the straighter edges.

The number of Chinese clothes in the Museum with stand-up collars like the one on this garment is small and those that do have this kind of neckline may be dated either to the second part of the last century or to the twentieth century. It seems probable that the style had a revival in China at this time, and may have been based on fashionable women's dress of the early seventeenth to the early eighteenth centuries, now only known to us through paintings. These show very high-necked collars fastened with two horizontal metal clasps, one on top of the other. [73] As the twentieth century progressed these collars became deeper, and so more like those 38 from the earlier period, as can be seen on another jacket, again made from velvet.

The high close-fitting collar is one of the hallmarks of the 'cheong sam' (chang shan)[74], that alluring twentieth century adaptation of the traditional woman's robe of China, whose western-inspired tailoring emphasizes the curve of the body. [75] It is from these hybrid garments that European women's dresses copied this type of collar to give an oriental touch to their fashions, and the collar is often referred to as a 'mandarin collar' by Europeans.

The 'cheong sam' in its final, evolved form was more like a dress in the European sense than a robe, whereas traditional garments, especially Han Chinese ones, were obviously to be worn as part of an ensemble. Here is how Chinese women appeared to one Englishwoman in the late nineteenth century:

On the following pages:
32 *Manchu woman's robe*, embroidery on twill weave silk, 19th century, 137 × 209 cm, T. 173-1961.

33 *Manchu woman's robe*, embroidery on twill weave silk, 19th century, 136 × 207 cm, T. 209-1948.

'A roomful of Chinese ladies presents a very pretty appearance, from the exquisite gradations of colour of their embroidered skirts and jackets, the brilliancy of the head ornaments, and their rouge… Their skirts are very prettily made, in a succession of tiny pleats longitudinally down the skirt, and only loosely fastened together over the hips, so as to feather round the feet when they move in the balancing way that Chinese poets liken to the waving of the willow'.[76]

The skirts she refers to would have been part of every well-to-do Han Chinese woman's wardrobe. They would have looked like the one illustrated here, made from two separate sections of green satin secured into a red cotton waistband and overlapping each other. Each section is composed of a straight, densely-embroidered and outlined panel, a pleated panel, and a narrower, almost unadorned panel. Only one of these unadorned panels is visible in the reproduction; the second is hidden by the overlap. When the skirt is worn, wrap-around style, both the plainer panels are hidden and the decorated straight panels are at back and front, with the pleats flaring out at the sides. The skirt has a pink silk lining, self-patterned with plum blossoms, chrysanthemums, narcissi, and peonies. The embroidery, both on the green satin and on the applied black trimming, is of high quality. Collectors' items and antique vessels, some of them filled with fruits and flowers, are intricately worked in rich multicoloured floss silk embroidery thread. Black satin cut on the cross is used to edge the entire garment and to highlight the pleats, while an applied woven ribbon further defines the panels and hem.

Three-quarter length robes whether side-fastening or front-fastening would be worn unbelted over skirts like this, hiding the skirt's waistband and undecorated portion. The western idea of a shapely silhouette, accentuating a particular part of the body as the fashion of the day dictated, was unknown in China until the twentieth century. There would be several layers of clothing beneath the skirt for

Below left:
38 *Woman's jacket*, black silk velvet on a mauve satin weave ground, early 20th century, 57 × 134 cm, T.5-1911.

Below right:
40 *Girl's jacket and trousers*, purple and white resist-dyed silk, early 20th century, jacket 90 × 140 cm; trousers 86.5 cm, T.124-1961.

warmth, extra bulk, and modesty. Skirts would have been bunched up around the waist or hips and secured with tape threaded through the two loops. No attempt would have been made to achieve a neat, smooth outline.

In the twentieth century some women wore their robes shorter and more close-fitting, rather in the style of a tunic. [77] A greater proportion of the skirt was consequently visible and the decorated area therefore increased. Perhaps copying a western idea, twentieth century skirts in this particular style often matched the tunic-like top both as regards materials and the embroidered designs. [78] This was not the case, however, with the skirts and robes of the type illustrated here. To European eyes the green skirt would not have matched the robe worn with it.

Despite the merging of clothing styles in the nineteenth century, it is doubtful whether Manchu women ever adopted skirts. As far as we can tell, skirts seem to have a purely Han Chinese line of descent, similar but simpler ones having been found in tombs dating from the first and second centuries B.C. Skirts made from two overlapping pieces of cloth, recovered from a mid-thirteenth century tomb, already seem to be identical with later examples. This site produced twenty women's skirts, plain and pleated, and mostly yellow in colour. [79]

For the Qing period it seems that older women wore dark blue, lilac, and mauve skirts while those for widows were black. The women's skirts in the collection date from the nineteenth and twentieth centuries and are of many different colours. They conform to the general style of the green skirt pictured here, with satin, a soft self-patterned silk and silk with a gauze weave design against a plain weave ground being the most common materials. Some of the skirts have closely-packed, sewn-down pleats resembling European smocking in appearance. These are called *yu lin bai zhe qun,* 'fish-scale, one hundred pleats skirts'. [80] Others are hardly pleated at all. The disposition of the applied edgings and ribbons varies from one skirt to another and winter ones are wadded and trimmed with fur. The rustle and swing of skirts such as these, accentuated by the gait imposed on the wearer by foot mutilation, was an important erotic element in the writings of male Chinese, and helped to reinforce an image of Chinese women as demure and subservient. [81]

A Han Chinese woman would wear trousers or leggings, sometimes decorated, beneath her skirt and at informal indoor gatherings she may have been invited to divest herself of the latter. [82] Otherwise, trousers were worn without a skirt only by young women and working women. They were not regarded as garments of emancipation as they were in some respects in the West. In keeping with other Chinese clothes trousers were not tailored to fit the waist or hips although one undecorated pair (T.2-1957) has elastic threaded through a turned over top. This must be a later alteration. These black trousers are very full and taper considerably towards the ankles. Two other pairs of Chinese women's trousers have jackets to match. As we have already noted this is not always the case with skirts. The fact that the two halves match may indicate a twentieth century date for the trouser suits. The size of both suits is commensurate with their having been made for young women, while the matching style may have been a particular fashion popular with this age group.

Fig. 2
40
41

41 *Girl's jacket and trousers,* blue and white resist-dyed cotton, early 20th century, jacket 69 × 105cm; trousers 59 cm, T.234-1966.

On the following pages, top:
34 *Woman's robe,* weft-patterned, early 18th century, 145 × 172 cm, T.187-1948.

Bottom:
36 *Han Chinese woman's robe,* silk velvet, late 19th – early 20th century, 98 × 123 cm, T.201-1934.

39 *Han Chinese woman's skirt,* embroidery on satin weave silk, late 19th – early 20th century, 101 cm, FE.12-1980.

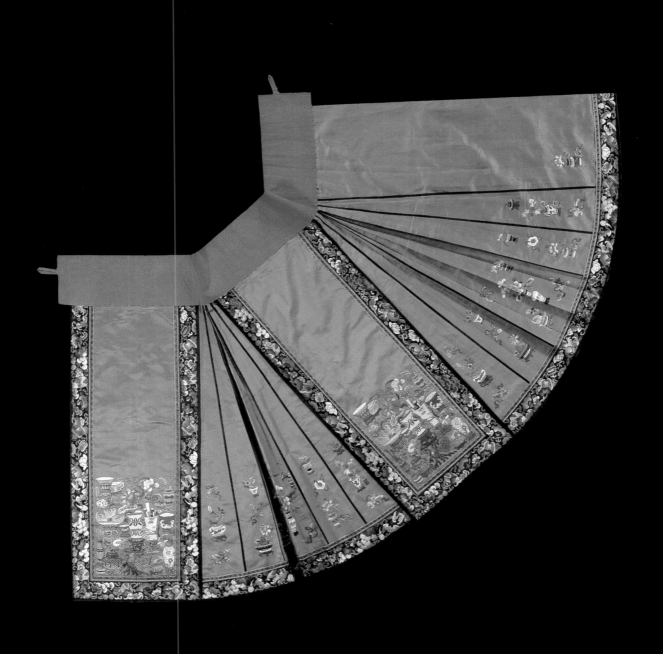

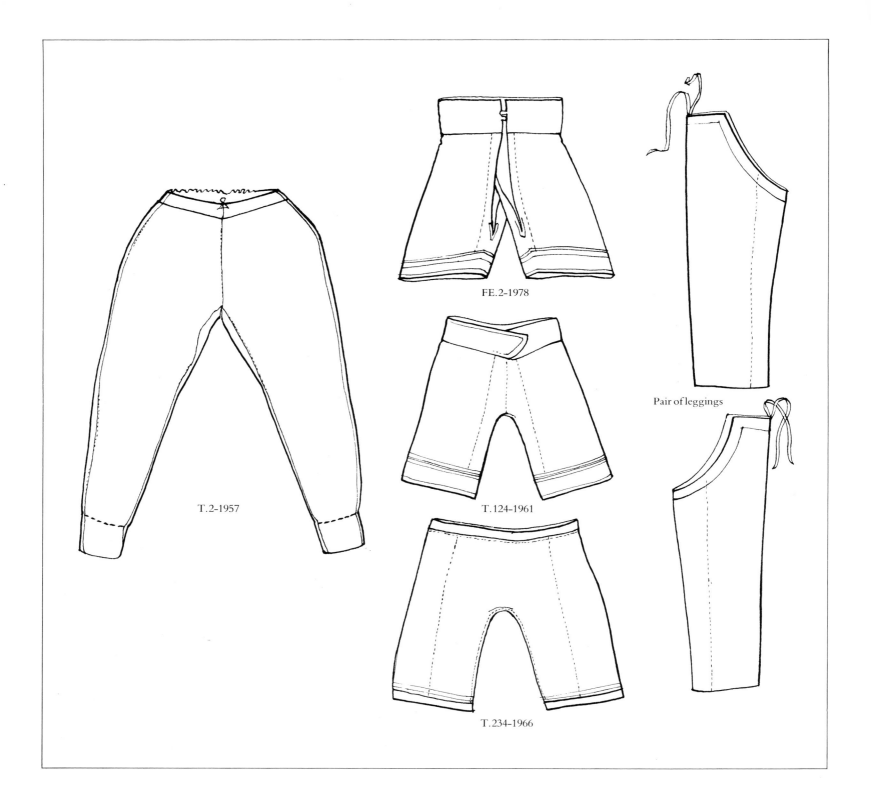

T.2–1957

FE.2–1978

T.124–1961

T.234–1966

Pair of leggings

The cotton trouser suit, coming from a household of moderate means and almost certainly made at home, was perhaps cut from an available piece of cloth which suitably accommodated both jacket and trousers. Except for a small number of garments from minority groups within China, this suit and a single larger jacket (T.233-1966) are the only cotton items of dress in the Chinese collection. The Museum purchased them from the Church Missionary Society, and they reflect the ability of European missionaries to penetrate levels of Chinese society unknown to casual visitors. Cotton production was widespread during the Qing dynasty (1644-1911), although by 1904 in Sichuan province the cotton plant was disappearing in the face of imports from India. [83]

The trousers and top have a design of fish, flowers and symbols representing one traditional view of the forces sustaining the cosmos. The pattern is achieved by laying a stencil onto natural-coloured cotton and pushing lime mortar or bean curd paste through the cut-out parts. When the paste hardens, the cloth is dipped into a dye bath and only those areas of cotton free from paste soak up the colour so that when the resisting paste is removed the design stands out against a coloured ground. [84] In this case, as on nearly all cotton clothes of this type, the background is blue, a colour commonly known as indigo and obtained from a substance called indican found in many different plants. Synthetic indigo was in use in Europe in the early twentieth century and it was quickly available in China. This paste-resist method of patterning was widely distributed throughout China and continues to the present day. The use of wax as a resist seems to be confined to non-Han minorities of the provinces of Guizhou and Yunnan. [85]

The bright purple trouser suit impeccably finished in every detail is also resist-dyed, a more unusual technique for garments made from silk. The silk is self-patterned with a small-scale design, invisible in reproduction, while the addition of resisted flowers on the jacket and butterflies and flowers on the trousers creates another layer of patterning. Coloured details have been painted on, much as they were on late Qing ladies' robes of silk tapestry. It may have been the intention to make the suit look as if it were woven in this expensive technique. In the event, the purple silk ensemble is more successful in achieving a clear design than many of the poor quality silk tapestry robes it perhaps sought to copy.

Fig. 2
Each pair of trousers mentioned so far is tailored in a different way, and these differences are best seen in the drawings showing their cut. The shortest pair in the Museum group is made along the same lines as a Chinese skirt, with overlapping
42 panels of yellow gauze weave silk sewn onto a cotton waistband. The bottom corners of each panel are sewn together for a depth of 10cm, so forming leg holes. When worn the long slit would be to the back. The trousers' short length, 53.5cm overall, suggests either that they were full-length trousers for a child, or possibly an item of women's underwear, the split back being a convenient style in either case.

36
Women's robes, together with the dragon robes, form the major part of the Chinese dress collection in the Victoria and Albert Museum. The blue velvet robe was probably worn by a Han Chinese woman and we have already quoted a description of the dress of such women (p. 52). On the other hand, Lady Hosie was

Opposite: Fig. 2 *Women's Trousers*

42 *Woman's undergarment or child's trousers, embroidery on yellow gauze weave silk, late 19th – early 20th century, 53.5 cm, FE.2-1978.*

probably describing Manchu women when she wrote:

> 'their long straight gowns fell to their ankles without a break in a shimmer of exquisite thick satin and brilliant hue, pure and delightful to the eye – amethyst, aquamarine and amber, with never an interruption in the colour save at the neck, cuffs and side openings where the finest embroidery concealed the fastenings'. [86]

It is interesting that Lady Hosie saw women dressed like this *after* the 1911 Revolution which ended the Qing dynasty. Although the garments of her Manchu acquaintances were plain, in other respects they may have been similar to a gown in the Museum illustrated on the front cover. Its length, 136cm from the back of the neck to the bottom of the hem, certainly makes it Manchu in style. This type of women's long garment is called a *qi pao* in Chinese, *qi* meaning 'banner', (a colloquial term for 'Manchu') and *pao* meaning 'robe'.

Many nineteenth and twentieth century women's gowns, both Han Chinese and Manchu, were lavishly decorated on the main body of the garment as well as on the trimmings. It seems that embroidered garments had been fashionable for women from the end of the seventeenth century when Ye Mengzhu noted the changeover from woven to embroidered designs. [87] These earlier garments would not have been so heavily trimmed as the deep pink robe. The richly-coloured background silk in a twill weave is embroidered predominantly in satin stitch with flowering sprays and bulbs, butterflies and peaches. The whole garment is set off with four edgings, a plain black bias-cut satin, the same black satin densely embroidered and two polychrome woven ribbons of different widths. The tuck in the wider of these two white-ground ribbons just below neck level at the front is characteristic of many of these ladies' robes. The ribbon itself follows round the narrow black binding of the collar. It then has to be pleated over in order for it to continue outlining the sloping band down towards the armpit, because, at the centre seam, the narrow black binding is taken up and around the top of the curving embroidered band. This may seem a clumsy tailoring device to ensure that the ribbon is always applied at the same distance from the next row of edging since there are examples where the ribbon application is effected more smoothly. It is likely, however, that the style is one of those small elusive fashion notes. Lack of Chinese dress documentation makes it impossible for us to pin down the exact time of its popularity. The straight sleeves of this garment are lined with white satin embroidered with the same motifs as those on the deep pink ground. This lining extends all the way back to shoulder-level, perhaps giving the wearer the option of turning back the sleeves to reveal white cuffs.

This Manchu robe is just one example of a garment having a near-identical counterpart either within the Victoria and Albert Museum or in collections elsewhere. We know that robes could be purchased off-the-peg in the nineteenth and twentieth centuries. [88] It is therefore reasonable to assume that similar robes may have been made in the same workshops, or else may have marked the style of a particular place.

Another full-length woman's garment is of bright blue twill weave silk with black satin edgings and ice blue satin cuffs. Plainly the robe was carefully conceived

as a whole, the design of flowers, bats and 'long life' characters extending across all the silk surfaces. The characters are embroidered throughout in bright purple and stand out sharply from the shaded silvery tones which are used for the other motifs. The narrow black binding follows the same course around the neck and curved closure as on the previous robe, and the curled cut-out shapes at the top of the side seams are also like those on the deep pink robe. Unlike the pink robe, however, this robe has no applied woven ribbon to interrupt the coherent design.

45   A three-quarter length robe in Han Chinese style also lacks lavish ribbon and embroidered edgings. Even their more modest use around the neck and sleeves may indicate a late nineteenth century application, the garment itself probably dating from around the first part of that century. The ground satin is evenly dyed a rich deep blue. The delicately-embroidered design consists of different rural

44 *Manchu woman's robe*, embroidery on blue twill weave silk, late 19th – early 20th century, 132 × 136 cm, T.231-1948.

59

Top:
45 *Han Chinese woman's robe*, embroidery on dark blue satin weave silk, early 19th century with later trimmings, 104 × 144 cm, T.217-1948.

Bottom:
46 *Han Chinese woman's robe*, embroidery on pale green twill weave silk, late 19th century, 122 × 141 cm, T.230-1948.

60

vignettes contained within roundels and spread across the hem. In some instances the separate landscape elements are out of scale with each other.

46   On another example unusually large motifs, 25cm high, are spaced across a pale green twill silk ground. Figure representations are not commonly found on Chinese dress, and these are all the rarer for their size. The flower carrying immortal maidens are dressed in beribboned costumes, the eclectic style of which places them in a nebulous utopia. This bold design, without a landscape reference, and the ornate and meticulous embroidery are more often associated with decorative hangings than with clothes. This is the only robe in the Museum's collection that is seamed along the shoulders, perhaps indicating that the material was originally destined for a different use. The side and shoulder seams are machine sewn, while the central ones are seamed by hand.

Sleevebands and Applied Edgings

There are no Chinese stitch samplers. Perhaps it is reasonable to suggest that in
47 China embroidered sleevebands sometimes served a similar purpose to European samplers. Sleevebands survive in collections throughout the world in very large numbers. Many of them were never used and some of them were left unfinished.

Sleevebands were applied as cuffs to women's robes. A great many of them were of white, cream or pastel coloured silk satin, suggesting that their function was purely an aesthetic one of contrast with the darker robe. Although many items embroidered for the European market were executed on this pale satin, it is unusual to find entire robes made from it, perhaps lending some credence to the view that white was mostly reserved for mourning (p. 81). The sleeve-bands pictured here show the range of decorative motifs used by the embroiderers. The pair on the left depict Chinese warriors in the conventionalized manner also found on ceramics and lacquer of the nineteenth century. As we saw earlier, decoration involving human figures is generally rare on Chinese dress, sleevebands being the principal exception to this. Sleevebands, as exemplified by this pair, do not necessarily have identical designs on them. Here, each band is treated as a separate decorative field. The two middle pairs show the common motifs of peaches, butterflies, flowers and rocks, all elements from the decorative repertoire long since leeched of any real significance. The pair on the right have garden pavilions embroidered on them in the manner Europeans associated with the 'chinoiserie' style. An inscription over the moon gate at the top reads 'Cavern Heaven', originally a term denoting Taoist paradises in the bowels of the earth. By the time these sleevebands were made in the nineteenth century it had become a clichéd name commonly applied to garden architecture. Whereas western samplers often have the embroiderer's name and the date of completion stitched into the design, Chinese sleevebands only ever bear inscriptions of the kind shown here or, occasionally, stanzas of poetry. The embroiderers remain anonymous. Embroidered sleevebands far outnumber those in other techniques although velvet and woven silk tapesty ones are seen. It is important to note that the sparseness of the evidence for treating them as items of domestic embroidery should leave us open to the consideration that at least some of them may have been made by professional workers.

When studying a blue velvet robe earlier we mentioned the other kinds of trimmings besides sleevebands that were often used to adorn women's dress (p. 49). The front-fastening jacket pictured here has no embroidered sleevebands. 48 Instead, the cuffs are marked by two coloured ribbons, the narrower of which is also used to outline the neck, front and jacket bottom. As this garment was designed to be worn in addition to a long robe the sleevebands on the latter would probably have extended beyond the jacket sleeves.

There was a sharp increase in the manufacture of this silk ribbon in the second half of the nineteenth century according to the commission of enquiry into silk conducted by the Imperial Maritime Customs. For example, in Nanjing before 1850 there were 'only a few score looms' while after that date there were 3,000 looms capable of producing 300 different ribbon patterns. The widths of these Nanjing ribbons were reported as being between two and three inches. This measurement is at variance with the ribbons applied to garments in the Victoria and Albert Museum's collection. The widest Museum example is much less than two inches but as ribbon seems to have been made in other parts of China, narrower widths may have been produced elsewhere. Suzhou and Shanghai figure as large ribbon producers and although the names of the patterns are recorded the widths are not. [89] John Henry Gray saw silk edgings for Chinese ladies' dresses being woven and sold in Canton. [90] Chinese ribbon from Canton, Hangzhou, Ningbo and Suzhou was displayed at the Vienna World Exhibition in 1873. It was thought by one knowledgeable observer to reveal a 'negligence dans le tissage'. [91]

Opposite:
47 *Sleevebands for women's robes*, embroidery on satin weave silk, late 19th – early 20th century, max. length of decorated area 59 cm, (left to right) Circ. 786/7-1912, T.114-1948, T.211-1957, Circ. 807/8-1912.

Below:
48 *Woman's jacket*, embroidery on dark blue satin weave silk, wadded, late 19th – early 20th century, 65 × 137 cm, T.125-1966.

62

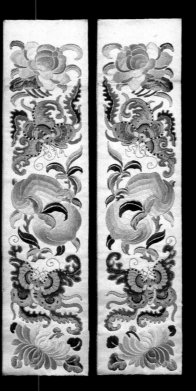

Consul-General Hosie gives an explanation of ribbon weaving as he saw it being done in Sichuan province. Silk braiding and round silk cord making were also observed by Hosie although he does not tell us what the final products were used for. [92] The braid manufactured in Shanghai seems to have been put to a similar use as the ribbon edging, but if we are to take the term 'braid' to mean a narrow fabric with threads laid together in a diagonal formation then the women's robes in the Museum's collection do not seem to be decorated with such trimming. Plaited gold-wrapped thread is found as a border on some dragon robes but on the kind of women's dress we are discussing here a plain or satin predominantly warp-patterned ribbon is usual.

The European official of the Imperial Maritime Customs when compiling his report on the Shanghai area for the silk commission distinguished between ribbon and braid. However the Chinese term used alongside the two English terms is the same in both cases. *Lan gan* has the primary meaning of 'railing' or 'balustrade'. Such decorative woodwork was used to edge the verandahs of garden buildings and the term provides an insight into how such patterned fabric edging was viewed by its makers.

49   The sleeveless top shown here is trimmed in a manner characteristic of late nineteenth century Chinese women's clothes. Three different borders set off the main dark blue panel of coloured and gold embroidery. The inner border is a narrow ribbon of the type described above. Next to this, is a wider band

Below left:
49 *Woman's or girl's overgarment*, embroidery on dark blue satin weave silk, late 19th– early 20th century, 39.5 cm, T.110-1964.

Below right:
50 *Manchu woman and her servant*, by C.H. Graves, 1902.

embroidered in gold, white and shades of blue. The exclusive use of blue, very typical of these trimmings, is hard to account for. It may have been appealing for reasons of fashion, or it may have something to do with the traditional use of indigo for dyeing. Possibly economics may have played a part too. The third border is a bias-cut black satin edge. On this top the applied decoration accords with the garment's shape. Only at the neck is the broad sweep of trimming interrupted by the straight front panel.

On many items of Chinese women's dress there is an over-abundance of these trimmings which encroach upon the main garment pieces, sacrificing the harmony of the whole as can be seen in an early twentieth century photograph of a Manchu lady wearing such a jacket. These sleeveless overgarments could be front-fastened, side-fastened or have a completely detachable front for ease of dressing. All of them are exceptionally wide to accommodate the robe beneath, and some of them are almost full length. These long sleeveless coats are perhaps associated with Han garments and the short ones with Manchu dress. [93] It is doubtful whether this division was strictly adhered to in late Qing times. When we discussed garment cut, sleeveless jackets were mentioned as being more likely to have derived from skin garments than were dragon robes (p. 21). The case for these jackets having skin ancestors is strengthened by the fact that they are seamed along the shoulders. This may mean the prototype was a garment made from two skins, one for the back and another for the front joined at shoulder level. [94] In any case the armholes on all these sleeveless overgarments are generously cut, not so much because of an earlier hide tradition, but because it was necessary to ensure ample space for the main robe's deep sleeves.

Accessories for Women

Smaller items of adornment complementing the main dress were very much a part of Chinese fashion. Although the emphasis may have been different, there were as many accessories in a Chinese woman's wardrobe as in that of her well-dressed European counterpart.

Hats and caps were not considered modish essentials and were only worn when travelling, by Chinese working women and by the elderly among the élite. However the straight black hair common to nearly all East Asian women gave every opportunity for elaborate styling, and the pins and clips needed to secure such styles provided scope for further embellishment. John Thomson, one of the most sympathetic Victorian recorders of the Chinese scene, took a series of photographs which show variations in ladies' coiffures throughout the different provinces of China, noting in his lavish four-volume *Illustrations of China and its People* that false hair was in common use. The hair was only dressed once or twice a week and the gummy oil used to set it was obtained by soaking the wood shavings of a resinous tree in water. [95] Four watercolours from a set likely to have been influenced by Thomson's work give us some idea of the range of inventiveness in hairdressing. During the nineteenth and early twentieth centuries Han Chinese women favoured

65

此是姑娘頭搭拉蘇

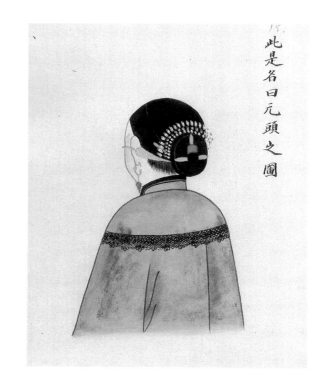

此是名曰元頭之圖

此是在旗兩把頭後面

此是在旗高把頭

54 smoothed down hair with fringes and partings. They wore elaborate knots or plaits at the back and sometimes at the sides as well, and as plates 51 and 52 show, these were often tied with decorative bindings and pinned with artificial flowers. The painting of a lady holding a mirror shows an unmarried girl's hairstyle, while the back view of the 'Round Head' style shows one for an older woman.

The different styles often had picturesque names. The 'Magpie Tail' style is included in the Museum's set of watercolours, and in the novel *Lao Can you ji* ('The Journeys of Lao Can') (1910) one character wears her hair in the 'Falling-from-Horse' style. Her sister's hair is adorned with a trembling
55 leaf-shaped ornament made from kingfisher feathers. [96] Several ornaments of this kind are illustrated here. We do not know whether they were worn as a set. The oval pieces containing coloured glass in the centre of the photograph are puzzlingly described in the Museum registers as 'cap buttons'. They were not used as buttons in any practical sense but were sewn onto silk bands worn around the hair line.
80 Sometimes the band would be embroidered or worked with pearls. Some were
91 pointed between the eyebrows like those worn by the women sewing pictured later in this volume. A custom commonly followed in the south of China was that of wearing natural flowers in the hair. The sprig was inserted into a small tube, the tapering end of which was pushed into the bun. [97]
53 The watercolours in plates 53 and 54 show two Manchu women with the 'High
54 Handle' style and the 'Two Handle' style. A front view of this latter style is seen in the photograph of a seated Manchu woman and her maid. The heavy wooden foundations necessary to achieve this look often caused headaches, and Lady Hosie noted the relief felt by some Manchu women at being able to put away these headdresses in the years immediately following the founding of the Republic in 1911. [98] It seems, however, that this cumbersome coiffure did not disappear altogether at this time. The construction on top of the head became twice as large as it had been at the beginning of the nineteenth century and it was seen as late as the 1920s and 1930s piled with exaggerated decoration. [99] The time spent coaxing the hair into these complex styles meant that Han Chinese and Manchu women of the upper classes spent as many hours as did wealthy Europeans in getting dressed. For such women personal maids were always on hand. The majority of the population settled for something simpler.

The maids must also have assisted with the mask-like face make-up. The ointments and powders, some of them, like white lead, having long-term detrimental effects on the skin, were kept in a brass or silver-bound wooden dressing case with a mirror in the lid. The face was first polished with a hot, damp cloth, the eyebrows trimmed, and any superfluous hair on the cheeks, neck and forehead was removed with two fine silk cords acting as pincers. Whitener was put all over the face, which was then highlighted with rouge. This came in the form of a small book with each leaf coated in red dye. The colour came off on a dampened finger which was then used to apply the tint to the face. [100] The eyebrows were thinly pencilled in and the lips painted in such a way as to make the mouth appear small and rounded. Petals of the balsam flower *Impatiens balsamina* were used in

Opposite top left:
51 *Hairstyle*, watercolour on paper, c. 1900, from a volume 23.5 × 17.8 cm, E.3301-1910.

Top right:
52 *Hairstyle*, watercolour on paper, c. 1900, from a volume 23.5 × 17.8 cm, E.3312-1910.

Bottom left:
53 *Hairstyle*, watercolour on paper, c. 1900, from a volume 23.5 × 17.8 CM, E.3307-1910.

Bottom right:
54 *Hairstyle*, watercolour on paper, c. 1900, from a volume 23.5 × 17.8 cm, E.3313-1910.

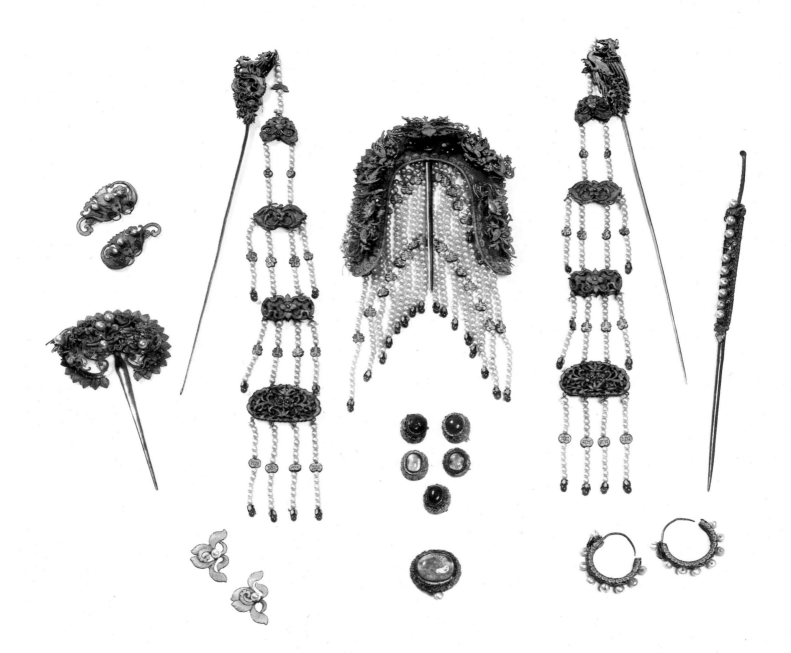

combination with alum to stain ladies' fingernails red. [101] Decorative nail protectors were worn by those who cultivated extra long nails.

Most women wore earrings, and if we are to judge by the watercolours and surviving photographs the pendant variety were more common than studs. Bangles and finger rings were also worn. They were principally made from silver, jade, opaque glass, carved lacquer or enamelled metal. Like some Chinese tailors, itinerant silversmiths were called to the richer private houses to make items of jewellery to order. [102] Beaded necklaces, apart from those associated with dragon and court robes, were seldom worn. Silver neckbands were the preferred type of neck ornament, but they seem to have been less popular than other items of jewellery. Strings of fragrant beads were, however, looped over robe fastenings, as

50 were carved jade pendants and sometimes abstinence plaques (4375-1901). These signified that the wearer was refraining from taking certain foods as an act of religious devotion.

Although we have referred to collars before, we should mention them again here since the detachable ones can be classed as accessories. As such, they presumably

56 could have been worn with different sets of clothes. These scalloped collars, skilfully cut in a manner reminiscent of Chinese papercuts, became a popular part of

Opposite:
55 *Jewellery*, kingfisher feathers, semi-precious stones on metal, acquired from the Amsterdam Exhibition in 1883, max. length 22 cm, 1237/38/40/44/45/46/67-1883.

Below:
56 *Collar*, embroidery on pale blue satin weave silk, late 19th – early 20th century, max. dimension 69 cm, Circ. 192-1910.

57 *Manchu women's shoes*, embroidery on satin weave silk, late 19th–early 20th century, top: 11 × 18 cm, 305, bottom 12 × 23.5 cm, 13055.

women's attire in the mid-seventeenth century. Their origins have been traced back several more centuries to Central Asia but all the surviving Museum examples date from the nineteenth century. [103] Instead of a collar, a long silk scarf was sometimes draped around the neck with one end secured under a button.

The shoes shown here represent just two of the many styles worn by Manchu women. Both are of satin, one embroidered with butterflies, the other with flowers. They are decoratively seamed and shaped at the toe end and are bound with black satin like the gowns. Additionally the shoe at the top has a tab at the back for easing it on. The shoes are lined with soft undyed cotton and have a stiff interlining. Several writers observed people pasting rags and paper into layers for shoe stiffening. [104] The wooden soles were heightened to give the wearer a grander appearance. More practically, these high shoes sometimes may have served to keep dress hems and feet out of the mud although it was unlikely that well-to-do women would ever have had to walk anywhere in inclement weather. Women learnt to accustom themselves to wearing such shoes and to managing their long gowns. The white lead used for ladies' cosmetics was also used for whitening shoe soles. [105] The embroidered uppers were often made by women at home, and these decorated parts were sent out to a professional cobbler to be made up. [106]

The Museum has examples of the tiny shoes worn by many women of the Han Chinese majority who had their feet deformed in childhood. Inside the shoes the feet were kept tightly bound with first bandages, and then broad ribbons. Gray saw many yards of this binding being woven. [107] As late as the 1930s an Englishman living in Tianjin could write home and relate how he was kept awake by girls of six years old crying through the night because their broken and bound toes were so painful. [108] A generation earlier Mrs Little had founded the Natural Foot Society while living in Peking. She travelled round China with examples of unnaturally small shoes as aids in her lecturing campaign against this brutal custom. [109]

Chinese robes were made up without pockets and prior to the twentieth century it was not the custom for women to carry handbags. Rich members of society had little need to carry anything, as they were waited on by servants, but it seems likely that personal items were transported in small purses and pouches, with folding fans and chopsticks carried in suitably-shaped receptacles. These were probably secreted in ladies' sleeves as they are hardly ever visible in contemporary watercolours or photographs.

Children's Dress

A serious study of children's clothes of any culture is always worthwhile, not least for the light it throws on the social and cultural habits of the time. The lack of a comprehensive range of children's garments precludes such a study for China within the Museum and we shall only briefly concern ourselves with the secondary sources. A two-volume watercolour album depicting boys playing shows the younger ones wearing side-fastening jackets while the older ones wear long gowns

Above:
58 *Pouch, embroidery on cream satin weave silk, late 19th – early 20th century, 25.5 × 9.5 cm, T.132-1963.*

Opposite:
59 *Fan cases and chopstick holders, late 19th – early 20th century, max. length 31 cm (l to r) velvet T.251-1948, embroidery T.153-1909, embroidery T.248-1912, embroidery 256-1866, embroidery T.152-1909, appliqué Circ. 283-1921, wang xiu embroidery Circ. 303-1930.*

60 like their fathers. All wear trousers narrowing at the ankle, although the small boy
61 in the painting of a mid-nineteenth century interior seems to be wearing them
loose. We have already noted that the slit pair of trousers in the Museum's collection
42 may have been intended for a child, and as the embroidery and edging are similar to
those on women's garments it seems likely to have been for a girl. The majority of
Chinese children's clothes in the Museum are for boys. It is indicative of the
attitudes of Chinese society that most of the watercolours painted by Chinese
62 artisans for export to Europe show male children. Photographs taken both by
visitors and resident European professional photographers, however, include girls.

Four small garments approximating, to a greater or lesser degree, to the adult
dragon robe (T.9-1923, T.182-1948, T.84-1969 and T.229-1948), and a court robe
for an infant son of a noble family (T.27-1950) demonstrate the practice, certainly
not unique to China, of turning children into miniature replicas of grown-ups. [110]
However, there is evidence in the Museum collection that some concessions were
made to youth. The humorous rendering of the embroidered animals on a
collection of pouches (T.112-1948) and on the front section of a small-size sleeveless
garment (T.119-1948) point to their having been made with children in mind. The
49 amusing clock buttons must have especially appealed to children although the
63 overgarment to which they are sewn could have fitted a small adult.

Sewing for children was part of the domestic round for most Chinese women.
Those who had leisure and wealth created something more than the merely
serviceable. One of Lady Hosie's Chinese acquaintances was sewing velvet shoes
quilted with cotton wool for the newest baby. Each shoe was shaped like a cat's
head and the tail at the back was weighted with a coin to help pull the shoe on. [111]

Patchwork, not a common technique in East Asia except for repairs and for

60 *Boys playing*, watercolour on pith paper,
c. 1860-1870, from a volume
15.5 × 10.5 cm, 8146.

Opposite top:
61 *Interior scene*, watercolour on paper,
c. 1850, 65 × 40 cm, D.23-1898.

Opposite bottom:
62 *Children at a mission school*, early 20th
century.

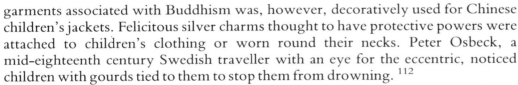

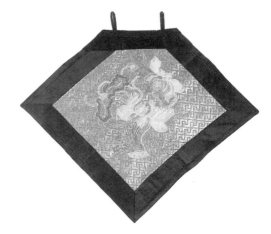

garments associated with Buddhism was, however, decoratively used for Chinese children's jackets. Felicitous silver charms thought to have protective powers were attached to children's clothing or worn round their necks. Peter Osbeck, a mid-eighteenth century Swedish traveller with an eye for the eccentric, noticed children with gourds tied to them to stop them from drowning. [112]

64 A baby doll – the Door of Hope missionaries who sent it from China around 1917 stressed that it represented a middle-class baby – with detachable clothes shows it wrapped in a wadded cotton blanket wearing slit trousers with feet all in one, a side-fastening top and a stiff collar. The bonnet-like hat completely covers the ears and back part of the head. The strong coloured cottons and silks used for Chinese baby clothes are quite different from the traditional knitted pastels of the western
65 layette. Sometimes an enlarged bib, roughly diamond in shape, was a Chinese baby's only covering.

Men's Dress and Accessories

The survival of so many dragon robes in museum collections tends to give us a false impression of Chinese men's dress in the nineteenth and twentieth centuries. While it is true that at certain times many people wore the dragon robe ensemble, it is also a fact that the aura which up till now has surrounded it made it more attractive than everyday dress to those foreigners wishing to possess something they thought to be uniquely Chinese. Although western collections may tell us otherwise, the majority of the male population of China did not own dragon robes. It is the Museum's loss that the softer-hued damask gowns and jackets worn by gentlemen of the Chinese upper classes, and some of the simpler hand-spun cotton clothes were overlooked in favour of ill-executed dragon robes with debased designs.

We should not assume, because the nuances which go to make up a particular period style are now mostly lost to us where China is concerned, that changes in fashion played no part in the choice of men's clothes. With such a narrow range of men's garments in the collection, they seem unchanging to western eyes, but there is enough literary evidence to prove that this was not so. The eighteenth century poet Yuan Mei found that the style of hat and robe he had worn when younger had come full circle again, and thirty years on was fashionable again. [113] A robe of wild mulberry silk, stylish in 1640 when Fang Yizhi, a writer and thinker, gave it to a friend, was felt to be old-fashioned and unwearable by 1646. [114] There were various style guides printed throughout the Qing dynasty for those who had the money and inclination to be trendsetters. For example, the *Da Qing sui shi ji sheng* ('A Record of the Flourishing of the Seasons of the Year') published in the mid-eighteenth century, amongst other up-to-the minute information, gives advice on where to buy the best clothes and on what to wear in which seasons. [115] A member of the Manchu aristocracy writing between 1817 and 1826 tells us that rose pink succeeded sky blue as the colour to wear in the 1760s, and around the 1780s a famous general named Fukang'an (d. 1796) started a fashion for dark red. The shade of red was called 'Fu red' after him. In the early nineteenth century ochre yellow and pale grey were the fashionable colours. [116]

Having few extant examples to guide us, we get most of our information regarding men's dress from contemporary photographs and paintings. However, a set of dolls now in the Bethnal Green Museum of Childhood gives us a good idea of the plainer style of dress favoured by upper and middle class Chinese men early in this century. The design of flowers on the self-patterned silk is outsize for such small clothes, but apart from this, we can be sure that the dolls are accurately dressed. They were sent from Shanghai by the Door of Hope Mission, and were made expressly to show the faithful back in England the different stations of life within the Chinese community.

Men wore ankle-length gowns cut, tailored, and fastened along the same lines as those for women. As we have seen, they were sometimes worn with a belt, which women's garments never were. It is hard to distinguish between Manchu and Chinese men's dress but it seems that Manchu men favoured the horsehoof cuff and that on gowns without dragon patterns these were turned back to reveal a lining of a different coloured silk from the rest of the garment. Like women, men often wore short jackets and sleeveless waistcoats over their long gowns. Close-fitting caps with a decorative silk knot on top and in the twentieth century western-style trilbys were worn with this type of clothing. The length of a man's gown marked out his

Opposite:
63 *Detail of 49.*

64 *Baby doll*, early 20th century, 30.5 cm, T.83-1936.

65 *Bib garment*, embroidery on stiffened gauze weave silk, early 20th century, 25 × 25 cm, Circ.777-1912.

75

place in society. In a short story by Lu Xun, one of twentieth century China's most famous literary figures, the customers in a wine shop are divided between the wealthier patrons, *chuan chang shande* or 'those who wear long clothes', and the *duan yi bang,* the 'short clothes group'. [117]

Manual workers wore a short, usually cotton, version of the silk gown with 67 trousers beneath. These were cut loosely and could be worn rolled up or bound in at the ankle. It was customary for a worker to secure his plait of hair out of the way around his head. As seen in the picture of furniture workers reproduced here, many artisans went barefoot. Otherwise, men wore plain black cotton or silk shoes with quilted soles. They did not favour such a built-up style as Manchu women, although photographs do show men wearing decoratively-embroidered slippers which offset their plain robes. Split bamboo was woven into sandals, and the fibre from the coir palm was used for making rain shoes. [118]

Men, perhaps because of the comparative lack of decoration on their robes and the fact that they often wore a belt, outwardly displayed colourful pouches suspended from their waists. The number increased as the Qing dynasty progressed. [119] We do not know whether there was a difference between those for women and those for men, and it is also difficult to be sure if the different sexes used distinctive fans. What is certain, however, is that the majority of Chinese-made fans in the Museum's collection were not used by Chinese people at all. They were made specifically with the European market in mind and as such they have their 68 own unmistakable style. [120] The folding paper fans illustrated here, however, are typical of those used within China even though the calligraphy on the top fan was written in London, at the Fisheries Exhibition of 1885, by the Chinese ambassador. The other fan has stained bamboo ribs, the guards being decorated with a mother of

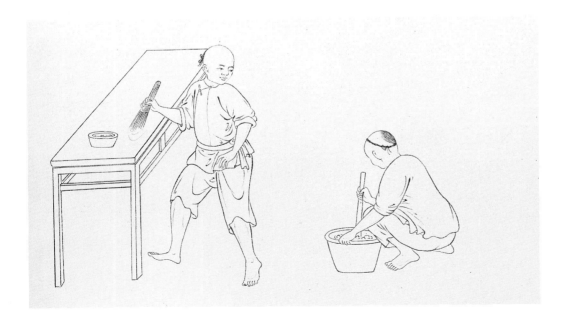

pearl inlay design of birds on branches of blossom. Both sides of the paper leaf have been dusted with mica to give a spangled effect and on one side is a painting of a traveller resting beneath a pine tree. The other side, shown here, bears a text describing the scenic and historic site of Luofu Shan, a mountain in Guangdong province famous for its Taoist and literary associations.

Pleated fans like this would concertina shut to fit into decorated silk cases. Many of these fan cases are bound with true braid as opposed to the ribbon edging found on Chinese women's garments. Rigid fans with handles in a variety of shapes and materials were used by both sexes. When they were not using them, men were able to tuck these into their belts, or into the top flap of their gowns.

The Museum has a varied collection of stoppered bottles and probably some of the smaller ones were carried around in drawstring bags by gentlemen who took snuff. Apart from official beads, male jewellery was limited to rings. These were sometimes worn on the thumb.

69

Other distinctive garments which we must mention in the context of Chinese men's dress are those robes with a detachable flap at the bottom right-hand side, armour, and military uniforms. The first, not represented in the Museum's collection although often depicted, were designed for mounting a horse easily. [121]

The Museum's suit of armour (T.205-1966) is not likely to have been worn in combat. Despite being studded with metal and having extra guard plates it would have afforded little protection on the battlefield and would have been worn as parade uniform by an officer. [122] It consists of a short jacket with horsehoof cuffs and a divided apron-like skirt. The foundation is of dark blue satin embroidered with dragon roundels, and this same fabric is used for the flaps surrounding the metal helmet. All the edges are bound with black velvet.

Opposite:
67 *Furniture workers*, ink on paper, c.1840, from a volume 30 × 30 cm, E.3184-1925.

68 *Folding fans*, paper and bamboo, top dated 1885, 31.7 cm, FE.33-1981. bottom dated 1882, 32 cm, FE.25-1980.

Above:
69 *Snuff bottles*, glass and hardstones, 19th century, max. height 7 cm, (left to right) 1500-1902, c.1571-1910, c.1735-1910, c.1925-1910, c.1764-1910, c.1938-1910.

On the following pages:
66 *Dolls representing a middle-class family*, early 20th century, max. height 30.5 cm, Misc. 80(1-3)-1969.

72 *Doll representing a hired mourner*, early 20th century, 30.5 cm, T.86-1936.

70 The Museum also has an example of the type of military jacket worn in the ranks. The insignia on the breast are those of a trooper in a detachment of the Left Wing of the Army of the Huai River stationed in Zhili province, the modern Hebei. The Army of the Huai River was one of several new armies equipped with more modern weapons and formed by the imperial government to fight the Taiping rebels in the middle decades of the nineteenth century. These armies continued to exist after the fall of the Taiping capital, Nanjing, to imperial forces in 1864. The jacket is made from bright blue hemp with applied wide bands of red, edged in a narrow white binding. Certain units of the Chinese Army adopted western-style uniforms from the mid-1890s.

The Revolution of 1911 marked the downfall of the Qing dynasty and the founding of a republic. Apart from the standard western suit with collar and tie which found favour with some Chinese men at this time, a high-collared centre-fastening jacket began to be seen in the 1920s. One name for it was a *xuesheng zhuang*, a 'student suit'. It probably derived, via Japanese student uniform, from a European prototype. [123] Dr Sun Yat-sen (Sun Zhongshan), the first provisional president of the Chinese Republic, became associated with this style. Even though he was not the first Chinese to wear it, it was sometimes called a *Zhongshan zhuang*, 'Sun Yat-sen suit', after him. What we now know in Europe as a 'Mao suit' after another illustrious wearer may have been influenced by this *Zhongshan zhuang*. The 'Mao suit', worn by Lenin and other revolutionaries in countries besides China, had a high buttoned pointed collar and breast pockets.

Qing clothing was not immediately abandoned in 1911. Lady Hosie tells us that in the tenth year of the Republic, 1921, many rich gowns were still seen. She cites as an example a Chinese gentleman who wore a beautiful floral damask robe lined

Below:
70 *Military jacket*, blue, red and white plain weave hemp, late 19th century, 74 × 160 cm, FE.1-1975.

Opposite top:
71 *Man's jacket and trousers*, blue self-patterned silk, wadded, post-1949, jacket 85 × 174 cm; trousers 127 cm, FE.94-1983.

Bottom:
73 *Woman's wedding skirt*, embroidery on red satin weave silk, late 19th century, 102 cm, T.182-1962.

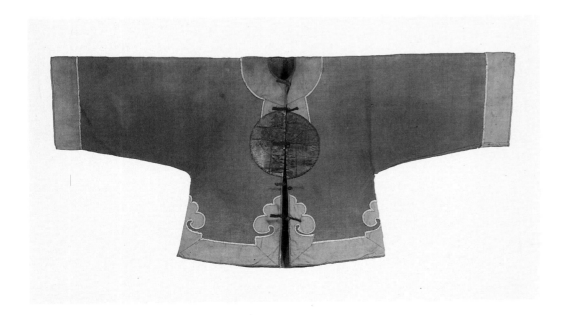

80

with expensive fur for a dinner engagement followed by a sixtieth birthday celebration. The gentleman in question was of the opinion that the Republic was the cause of so much fine dressing. 'Under the Great Pure Dynasty [ie. the Qing] it was considered bad taste for a gentleman or lady to wear finery at home or when visiting friends quietly. Now they constantly had to appear in new clothes'. [124] Traditionally-cut clothes of all sorts for both women and men continued to be worn up to the 1949 Revolution and some Chinese styles were worn after that date.

71   A post-1949 man's outfit shows the persistence of such styles into the latter half of the twentieth century, when this jacket and trousers were made. The generously-cut trousers, to be bunched in at waist level with a belt, and the button and loop-fastened jacket without shoulder seams are familiar eighteenth and nineteenth century Chinese garment shapes. This particular suit was made by a Chinese tailor for Sir John Addis (1914-1983) to wear while riding his bicycle around Peking when serving in the British diplomatic service there. It was made from silk which even in the austere years following the 1949 Revolution played a vital part in China's economy.

Special Occasions

Two ceremonial observances which universally demand special attire are weddings and funerals. A variety of clothes were worn by mourners attending the same funeral, the majority dressing in un-dyed or whitish-coloured garments. Although white was worn in the humid south of China at the height of the summer at times other than funerals nonetheless it does seem to be associated with death. [125] A completely unadorned robe made of coarsely-woven hemp (T.388-1967) came into the Museum's collection described as a protective covering for a court robe. It is cut in the full-skirted court robe style, but may in fact be mourning dress. A Door of 72 Hope Mission doll representing a 'Hired Mourner' is also dressed in a hemp robe, although of a very simple cross-over type.

    Weddings too generally required garments of a specific colour, in this case red. 73 The woman's wedding skirt shown here is made from six red satin panels and six streamers, all attached to a cotton waistband. The central panels back and front bear a design of a dragon and 'phoenix' respectively, and these, together with the wave pattern and craggy rocks are more commonly found on dragon robes (p. 12). The use of these motifs lent a seriousness to the occasion, as well as elevating the social standing of the bride. The streamers, two each of yellow, dark blue and light blue, are embroidered in different colours with flowers, butterflies and bats, and each is self-lined and has a floral spray embroidered on the reverse. Applied woven ribbon and black edging outline both panels and streamers and the hem is trimmed with a heavy green knotted silk mesh ending in long yellow tassels. Metal bells in the form of lotus pods are also attached to the hemline. The skirt is lined with red silk self-patterned with stylized foliage and the whole garment has been carefully and strongly made.

Han Chinese girls did not generally wear skirts or put up their hair until they were about seventeen years old. A skirt was essential on the wedding day. An entire set of red clothes could be hired for a marriage celebration. [126] The bride in the early-twentieth century novel *The Journeys of Lao Can* did not wear red, the common colour for all Chinese festive occasions, but a plum-coloured jacket, a 'sunflower green' gown, and a pale pink skirt. [127] All women were expected to marry unless they entered a religious order. In late traditional Chinese society there was no such thing as the revered spinster. Arranged marriages were not inevitably a disaster, but because of their extremely confined lives Chinese girls were often heartbroken to leave their childhood homes. Unfamiliar clothes on their wedding day must have added to their fears of a different life to come, especially when the bride's vision was severely restricted by a thick silk veil entirely covering her head and face. [128] Less imprisoning bridal veils were made from strings of pearls 74 suspended over the face from an ornate tasselled or pompom-decorated headdress. Manchu women may have copied some Han Chinese wedding customs. A standard dragon robe (T.220-1948), predominantly red, would not have been suitable for government business wear because of its colour (p. 118) and extra sleevebands. It may have been worn by a Manchu bride.

A Chinese bridegroom often wore a dragon robe or an approximation of one, even if he was not ordinarily entitled to this. Elaboration and fanciful interpretation of the standard dragon attire raised the groom to greater prominence on this 75 important day. A wedding hat for a man illustrates this kind of adaptation. Red silk sashes draped crossways over the shoulder and loosely knotted under the arms were also worn by bridegrooms and sometimes by attendants and guests as well. [129]

Theatrical and Religious Costume

A Chinese theatrical performance is an exuberant mix of dancing, singing, music and acrobats. The paucity of scenery on stage in all the various forms of traditional Chinese drama serves partly to point up the richness of the actors' costumes, which have their greatest impact when viewed from a distance. Although women perform today, in all but a few provincial styles of drama men traditionally took both male and female roles in Qing times. A character is immediately recognizable 76 by the costume he wears and the way his face is painted. The costume shown here, even though it has a design akin to that found on dragon robes, is marked out for theatrical use by its lavish use of gold work and its archaic cut. It is also outsize. It may have been a costume for a high official, one of the types which together with languorous young lovers, heroic generals, comic underlings and bossy old ladies dominated the repertoire. It is not possible to say whether this is a Peking Opera costume or one from the many regional styles.

The practice of robing devotional images in real textile garments is, of course, 77 not confined to China. These image robes are distinguished by their size, often being either far too big or too small for the human frame. Although not so heavily

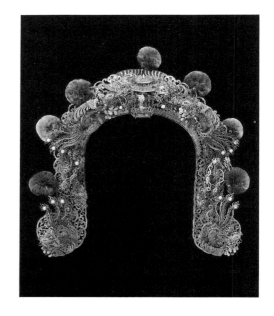

Top:
74 *Bridal headdress*, kingfisher feathers and pearls on metal, late 19th century, 30.5 × 30.5 cm, 1235-1883.

Bottom:
75 *Bridegroom's hat*, red silk with black fur brim, metalwork and semi-precious stones, late 19th century, 17 cm, FE.145-1975.

Opposite:
77 *Robe for a statue*, green brocaded silk, cyclical date equivalent to 1791 or 1851, 220 × 196 cm, T.752-1950.

embroidered with metallic thread as theatre costumes, they do have wide sleeves and are secured by ties, not buttons. Robes in this style may have been easier to manipulate when clothing an inanimate object, and this practical consideration helped to perpetuate the garment's archaic elements. They are lined with tough cotton or hemp to prevent the silk's early destruction against a wooden or metal statue. These garments sometimes assume an importance in the dating of Chinese dress as some of them have inscriptions painted onto the lining (p. 121).

78 Other garments which sometimes bear inscriptions are the robes worn by Taoist practitioners when officiating at rituals. The complex iconographical schemes embroidered on them will not be discussed here, but their simple cut recalls an earlier period than that represented by surviving robes, the shape of these vestments demonstrating the conservative nature of ceremony. These Taoist robes rest on the shoulder, their limited tailoring utilizing the full width of uncut silk. Two lengths of material, or sometimes four lengths if the material is not very wide, are used seamed together vertically, folded in half horizontally to form the shoulder line, and left open at the front. The lower part of the sides are sewn together leaving armholes, or rather hand-holes. Although these garments are technically sleeveless, the expanse of silk projecting over the edge of the shoulders serves to cover the arms. [130] Only one of the Museum's Taoist vestments has proper sleeves formed by cutting away the underarm section of silk and creating a curved seam from hem to wrist (1620–1901).

All these robes have a wide border applied round the edges, as well as a collar band. Like image robes they are mostly lined with hemp. The use of hemp and the minimally cut silk of these robes may accord with Taoist ideas about the spiritual value inherent in natural and unworked materials.

Underwear and Seasonal Variations

Given the Museum's bias towards decorated robes, it is not surprising to find that there is no underwear in the collection of Chinese dress, but information on this aspect of Chinese clothing is available from literary sources and the Door of Hope Mission dolls. Details of ladies' undergarments can be found in *Two Gentlemen of China*, where Lady Hosie describes the layers beneath the visible garment:

'First, there was the *tou t'ou* [*doudou* in the Pinyin transcription] a diamond-shaped piece of cotton material, something like an apron, for the front of the person, tied with strings that went round the waist and back again to the front and fastened round the neck by a silver chain stitched to its highest point. Flower told me that she and most people preferred a less grandiose string or tape, because the silver chain pinches the flesh, which I found to be uncomfortably true. The *tou t'ou* was of flowered black and white printed calico, but Aunt Kung wore Japanese flannelette as being warmer, Flower told me. Then came the inner pair of trousers, fitting fairly tightly down to the ankle, of flannelette, and fastened at the waist by a tape. The next thing to be put on was the inner tunic, again of flannelette, the long white sleeves being visible at the wrist when the lady is dressed.' [131]

65 The *doudou* was the same bib-like garment as was mentioned in connection with babies and it seems not always to have been worn as an item of underwear. Over these layers went the trousers, panelled skirt and hip-length gown. We know little of Manchu underwear but it was probably similar to the above. S. Wells Williams recounted with some distress although perhaps without much investigation into the matter how the Chinese had 'a paucity of linen in their habiliments' but he did concede to their wearing 'undershirts of flannel' at least in Canton. [132] This may, in fact, have been the flannelette more accurately recorded by Lady Hosie. This soft-spun cotton with raised fibres was more readily available and better suited to undergarments than woollen flannel would have been. The Door of Hope Mission dolls, both men and women, wear starched cotton underwear consisting of loose trousers and waist-length long-sleeved tops. They all have on silk leggings narrowing towards the ankle and attached by tape to another tape circling the waist. Ramie, often known as China grass and produced in quantity in China, was also used for undergarments. It is a linen-like fibre produced from the stems of *Boehmeria nivea*, a plant belonging to the nettle family.

The number, quality and kind of undergarments must have differed according to the wearer's means and mode of life. Arguably, the climate affected these unseen

Opposite:
78 *Robe for a Taoist*, embroidery on white and red satin weave silk, late 18th–19th century, 127 × 183 cm, T.254-1959.

On the following pages:
76 *Theatre costume*, raised gold embroidery on satin weave silk, early 20th century, 117 × 224 cm, T.45-1933.

81 *Dragon robe*, embroidery on satin weave silk with fleece lining, 19th century, 138 × 174 cm, T.198-1953.

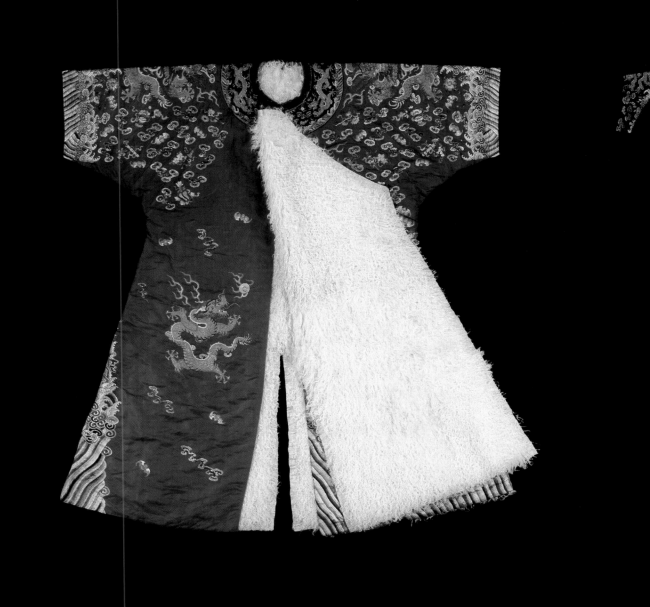

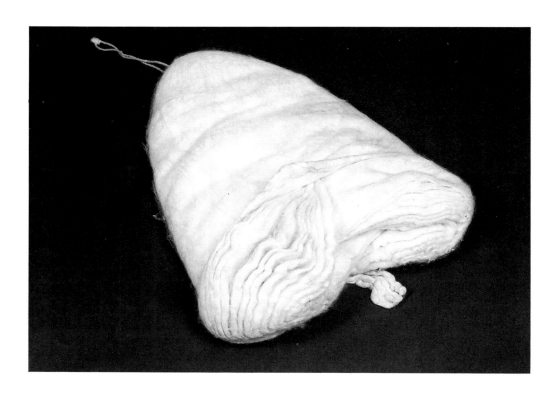

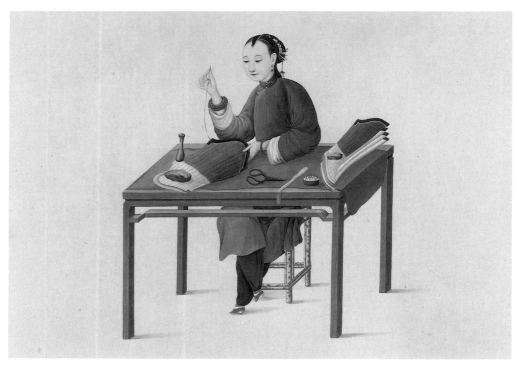

Top:
79 *Silk wadding*, 20th century, 46 cm,
FE. 28-1980.

Bottom:
80 *Woman sewing*, watercolour on paper,
c. 1790, 35 × 42 cm, D. 124-1898.

garments more than it did the robes worn on top. In summer, undervests made from short lengths of fine bamboo strung together were put on, and this prevented the other garments sticking to the skin. Hollow bamboo stems plugged with a sweet sticky substance acting as flea traps were also worn inside the clothes. [133]

China was and remains a country where in winter similarly-cut clothes are piled layer upon layer. These are subsequently peeled off as the weather becomes warmer. It was not the custom in the Qing dynasty to wear woollen or knitted clothing when it was cold. Silk and cotton remained the paramount fabrics in all seasons. Thus although the visible robe may have looked the same in summer as in winter those worn in the latter season were sometimes wadded or fur-lined, while those worn during the hotter months were often made from thin cotton or gauze weave silk. Because of its airy, openwork quality a plain weave thin cotton or silk robe would go underneath the gauze weave one.

The deep pink robe and the dark blue satin jacket, two garments we have looked at before (p. 58, 62), are both wadded. That is to say they have some kind of filling in between the lining and the outer silk. A cone of unused silk wadding is illustrated 79 here. Usually, in addition to the wadding, there is an interlining of tough, pliable paper to conserve heat and preserve the material. To prevent the wadding and paper from slipping down inside the garment, vertical lines of quilting are sewn through all the layers. There is no attempt to make these quilting stitches a decorative feature 71 and the thread used invariably matches the colour of the outer silk. Trousers for winter wear were given the same treatment ensuring the almost complete disguise of the wearer's shape. A watercolour shows this straight quilting being executed on 80 what appear to be the fabric uppers of soft boots, rather like spats.

As will have become obvious from the foregoing, the European conception of overcoats and outdoor clothes does not hold true for China. Fur, imitation fur made from Tibetan wool, cotton resembling a coarse towelling and sheeps' fleeces were all used as linings for garments which were worn both indoors and out in cold 81 weather. [134] Sometimes the fur was worn outermost. The choice of linings, like other dress details, was given careful consideration. In *The Journeys of Lao Can,* when one of the characters is given a fox fur gown as a present he feels it is too grand and does not accept it. One with a sheepskin lining would have been more suitable for a person of his class who habitually wore cotton clothes. [135]

Sleeveless overgarments should again be mentioned here for, although they became a fashion in their own right in the nineteenth century, they also served to keep out the cold. However, in keeping with the prevailing dress ethic of the time, these sleeveless jackets were not removed when the wearer went indoors.

The cloak, that often extravagant and extrovert fashion of the West, was not much worn in China. However, we know that the shape existed there and it perhaps qualifies as one of the few Chinese garments specifically designed to be worn out of doors. It seems to have been an informal item of dress worn by both sexes, but particularly by women, from the second half of the eighteenth century. It was colloquially called *yi kou zhong,* 'a bell' from its shape. [136]

Hand and foot warmers in the form of charcoal-fuelled miniature braziers kept the extremities warm. An implausible-sounding muff is recorded by Osbeck. He claims a live quail was carried in the hands in winter. [137]

Hoods were also worn during wintry weather, although the Museum's example, in embroidered silk satin, seems rather too flimsy to have kept out the cold (T.109-1964).

Buttons and Method of Closure

In the eighteenth, nineteenth and early twentieth centuries, button and loop fastenings were used to secure Chinese clothes. A narrow strip of silk, usually black satin, was formed at right-angles to one of the garment edges, leaving a loop at the end. A similar strip was sewn opposite this on the other edge. The closure is effected when the button attached to this second textile strip is secured through the loop in the first. Buttonholes are not found on Chinese garments, neither are eyelets for lacing, nor hooks and eyes, nor zip fasteners. Although flat buttons were used in China and some came in fanciful shapes such as teapots and clocks, the majority are spherical. Some of the ball-like buttons are plain and smooth and some have an irregular surface or openwork decoration. Apart from those buttons which are formed out of a firm knot of the same satin as is used for the strips, most of them are made from metal. John Henry Gray witnessed the making of one type of button in Canton in the 1870s. They were made by forming two halves of a ball with a punch and soldering them together. [138] In this case the metal used was copper. Tests carried out on buttons in the Museum confirm the use of this metal. In addition to copper minute amounts of zinc and traces of gold were also found to be present. These buttons could therefore be a cold gilded brass (an alloy of copper and zinc) or an homogeneous alloy of all three elements. In the case of some of the Museum samples, little blow marks may signify casting.

Button and loop closures were standard on both front-fastening and side-fastening garments. In the latter case both men and women buttoned their clothes to the right. During the period spanning the eighteenth to twentieth centuries with which we are concerned here the only Chinese who reversed this procedure were those who wished to make a political statement against the ruling dynasty at the time of the Taiping rebellion (1850-1864). [139] That this millenarian social revolution should place such emphasis on what from our perspective seems like a minor point of fashion reveals the powerful role of dress in China as a transmitter of cultural homogeneity. Otherwise the loops and buttons were spaced out along the right-hand edge of the gown overlap, one at the neck, one and sometimes two side by side half way along the collar bone, and then a straight line of three or four. There are no inside ties or closures but, as we have seen, belts were sometimes worn.

Women's front-opening coats, especially the longer and more shaped tunic type popular in the twentieth century (p. 53) sometimes had, in addition to buttons and

Fig. 3

Opposite: Fig. 3 *Button and Loop Closures*

Above:
82 *Perfume holder*, carved bamboo, late 18th century, 24cm, T.27-1909.

90

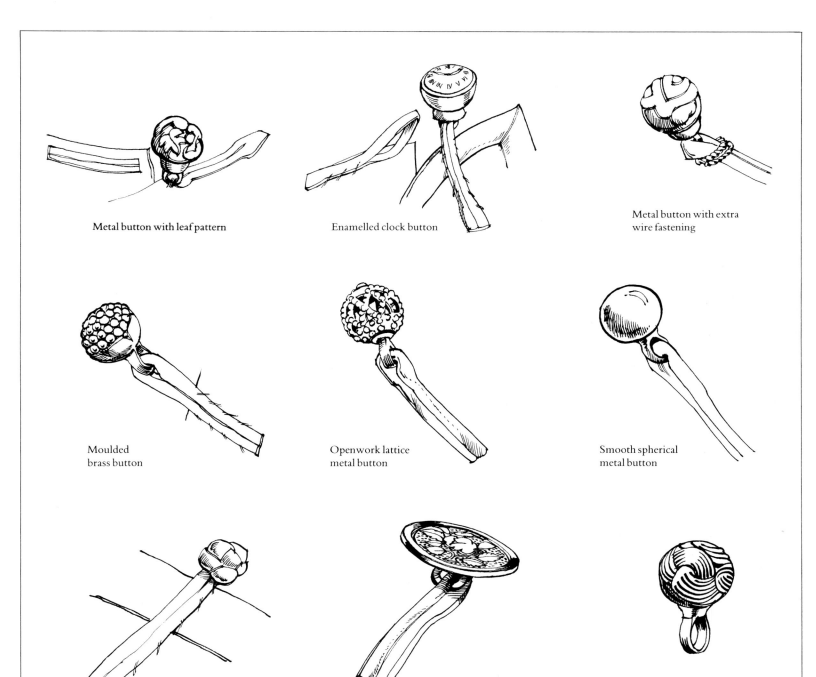

Metal button with leaf pattern

Enamelled clock button

Metal button with extra
wire fastening

Moulded
brass button

Openwork lattice
metal button

Smooth spherical
metal button

Button knot in satin

Flat metal button

Moulded metal button

sometimes instead of them, external silk ties which matched the coat fabric. Other garments which were fastened with ties only were theatre costumes and robes for religious images.

Chinese Traditions of Storage and Cleaning

Unlike the Japanese *kimono,* there seems not to have been a uniform way of folding Chinese robes. Nonetheless these straight-seamed garments were easy to store flat in chests and cupboards. They were never hung on hangers. Sandal and camphor woods, because of their pleasing fragrance and inherent insect-repelling qualities, were ideal for making furniture in which to store clothes. Otherwise carved 82 bamboo perfume holders could be inserted into the piles of clothing.

For cleaning, undyed or one-colour cotton garments could be safely immersed in water and washed with a brown native soap. This was made from the tallow found between the outer skin and inner membrane of the pods of a leguminous tree, *Gymnocladus chinensis,* which grows in central China. [140] It would not have been possible to wash the polychrome embroidered and woven silk garments because of the fugitive nature of the dye colours. Any form of weighting added to the silk during manufacture would also prevent washing. Except for some made from gauze weave, all the robes are lined throughout with plain or self-patterned silk, often in deep colours. These linings, and the winter interlinings, would provide an extra hazard if washing were attempted.

Some form of spot cleaning may have been carried out on fresh stains. In *The Story of the Stone* the maid Patience, undoubtedly high-ranking enough to wear silk, cries all over her dress. It is sprayed with rice wine and ironed with a flat iron. [141] Ironing was not carried out as a matter of course, and although the Manchu lady's 50 robe in the early twentieth century photograph reproduced here is crease-free, her servant's is very crumpled. The maid's more hurried life, requiring her to carry out awkward chores, resulted in her less-than-smart appearance. It seems not to have been expedient to give her gown a press even before posing for a photograph.

The Technology of Dress

Silk

In the preface to the *Yu zhi geng zhi tu* ('Imperial Pictures of Ploughing and Weaving'), a volume first published in 1712, the Kangxi emperor (r.1662–1722) encouraged farmers in sericulture and reminded court officials of the arduous labour involved in the production of their silk robes. Woodblock prints and accompanying text illustrate and describe the stages of silk manufacture. In spite of the book's idealized view of working conditions, each page reflects the different processes with some accuracy. The print showing a decorated altar with hanks of silk hanging above and gathered worshippers probably also closely depicts a real situation. In the mid-eighteenth century the Qianlong emperor (r.1736–1795) constructed a shrine to the patroness of silk in Peking. Silk held an important place in China's economy, and following the traditions of several past emperors, the annual sacrifice and the ritual raising and reeling of silk cocoons was an official imperial ceremony, presided over by the empress. Almost half the participants in the ceremony were women. The ritual deserves notice as the only public function for which women were made imperial officers. [142] No other industry was backed up by the state in this significant way.

The imperial silk shrine appears on Father Hyacinth Bitchurin's 1829 plan of Peking in the park with the distinctive bottle-shaped pagoda to the west of the imperial palace. By 1917 the altar was merely a tourist attraction, and by 1935 the ritual rearing halls were dilapidated. Although imperial involvement with the silk shrine had come to an end, worship organized by silkworkers themselves persisted. In the 1870s as the workers of one silk farm near Canton began work they dipped a mulberry branch into a basin of water that stood on an altar to the silk goddess and sprinkled themselves in a simple rite of purification. [143] A newspaper article published in 1934 reported that the Chinese government had turned down a request from the Society for the Improvement of the Silk Industry to set aside an official festival day for celebrating the patroness of silk. [144]

That the silk industry held an established place in China's economy during the Qing period, 'both as a source of primary goods and as an item of fiscal reckoning in the administration of the empire,' has been recorded elsewhere. [145] The botanist Robert Fortune, on his third visit to China between 1853 and 1856, was not able to gain information about the price of various silks without the Chinese immediately jumping to the conclusion that he wished to purchase some. [146] The vast range and quantity of surviving Qing silk garments is also evidence of the importance of this prestigious commodity. Today, even with improved strains of cocoon and more advanced processing techniques, 600 silkworms are needed to produce 1.7 square metres of silk cloth. [147] We can certainly believe in Fortune's estimate of 'millions of

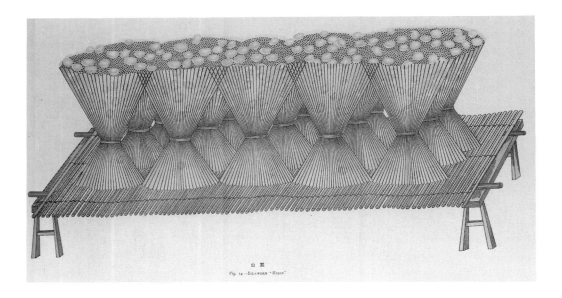

山蔟
Fig. 14—SILKWORM "HILLS"

cottagers' engaged in silk manufacture. In one town he found that even the poorest section of the population had at least one silk dress for best, proving that silk was not just the preserve of an élite. [148]

Millions of silkworms had to be sated with mulberry leaves so that the demand for silk could be satisfied. The Imperial Maritime Customs report of 1881 on the silk industry records the spread of mulberry plantations, and notes the practice of grafting the abundantly-leafing domestic variety onto saplings grown from seed of the hardy wild stock. [149] Fortune saw these grafted trees in the Lower Yangtze valley but not in south China. He describes how whole branches of foliage were expertly clipped from mature trees, allowing them to shoot up again though temporarily giving a wintry aspect to the landscape. [150] The considerable quantity of leaves produced solely for selling to silkworm rearers and the existence of 'green-leaf firms' *(qing ye hang)* or mulberry leaf brokers do not necessarily indicate that all the silk production was on a large scale such as Thomas Allom saw in the 1840s. [151] Fortune's 'cottagers' supplemented their incomes by sericulture and during the silk season all available space, time and labour were given over to the exacting tasks involved. In one instance the halls and outhouses of a monastery were used for feeding silkworms. As the door to one of the halls was opened 'hundreds of thousands of little mouths were munching the leaves, and in the stillness around, this sound was very striking and peculiar.'[152]

These silkworms would have been *Bombyx mori* caterpillars. Other kinds of silkworm were reared in China but with the exception of *Bombyx mori,* which is reared on picked leaves, they were all pastured openly on growing leaves of various plants. All varieties however spin silk in a similar manner. The moth lays its eggs and the larvae hatch and begin feeding. As they grow they take on the familiar appearance of a caterpillar, more usually called a silkworm in the sericulture

Opposite:
83 *Sacrificing to the Goddess of Sericulture,* watercolour on silk, after *Imperial Pictures of Ploughing and Weaving* of 1712, 23.5 × 23.5 cm, D.1650-1904.

Above:
84 *Silkworm 'Hills',* from *Silk: Replies from Commissioners of Customs . . .*

祀謝

春前作繭市盛事傳西蜀此邦
享先蠶再拜絲滿目馬草褁玉
肌能神不為辱雖云事渺茫鮮
與民為福

process. When the silkworm has greatly increased both its size and weight – in modern China a silkworm is ten thousand times heavier at maturity than when it first hatches from the egg[153] – it swings its head back and, with a figure of eight movement, pushes out from the sides of its body two strands of silk. These merge together with the aid of a gummy substance called sericin. The silkworm winds the strands around and around itself to form the cocoon. In the nineteenth century supports in the form of specially prepared bundles of straw called *can shan,* 'straw hills', were provided for the cultured silkworms to spin their cocoons on. Apart from meticulous cleaning and careful temperature control by the sericulturist the life cycle of the moth proceeds in the same way both in its natural and cultured state. The next stage is the crucial one for obtaining usable silk for weaving into cloth. The silkworm changes into a chrysalis inside its cocoon and presently breaks through the silk network to emerge as a moth. This tearing of the cocoon spoils the continuous silk thread, so the sericulturist must intervene either by killing the chrysalis, usually with steam heat before it makes its escape, thereby preserving the cocoon intact, or by winding off the silk immediately.

84

85 *Plate showing silk reeling,* enamelled porcelain, after *Imperial Pictures of Ploughing and Weaving* of 1712, early 18th century, diameter 34.8 cm, C.424-1926.

The cocoon is unravelled – or reeled – into a long silk filament between three and six hundred unbroken metres or more in length. Shorter silk fibres from the beginning and very end of the cocoon are not discarded but spun into continuous lengths in the same way as wool or cotton. In China silk with the maximum shine was produced from live cocoons but for this the timing had to be very carefully judged and there had to be sufficient labour to effect the reeling in time. To start the reeling process the cocoons were put into pans of hot water, and bamboo combs were trailed across the surface to pick up the ends. Filaments from eight to twelve cocoons would be passed through an eyelet and the sericin would aglutinate, causing them naturally to adhere into one thread as they were reeled onto a foot-operated square wheel. Depending on the ultimate use of this reeled silk it would then undergo a selection of different processes. These processes, between reeling and setting up the loom for weaving, have been glossed over by otherwise reliable sources. Robert Fortune and John Henry Gray do not mention them, while the Maritime Customs report on silk serves only to emphasize the confusing array of practices prevalent in the different silk-producing districts of China in the latter half of the nineteenth century. The *Imperial Pictures of Ploughing and Weaving* include a depiction of what seems to be silk throwing – the name given to the twisting of silk filament yarns. Consul-General Hosie's report of the silk process as carried out in Sichuan province, although rendered less useful by imprecise terminology, gives a meticulous description of the different twisting processes. Throwing increases the yarn's tensile strength although it is possible to use silk without any appreciable twist for the warp or the weft. Hosie is also very careful to record the degumming process, reporting that the majority of silk had the sericin gum washed out of it 'after it had been reeled from the cocoon and made into suitable yarn', but before it was dyed and woven. This sequence would ensure the maximum lustre. He says that weft for satin weave was not degummed before dyeing. [154] This is not necessarily borne out by observation of the garments in the Museum's collection whether they are of satin or other weaves.

Imperial Silk Workshops

Until 1843 there was a 'Weaving and Dyeing Office', the *Zhi ran ju* in the capital, Peking. It was set up in the reign of the Kangxi emperor to produce textiles for the imperial court and we know that in 1751 it contained sixteen looms. *Duan,* 'satin', and *sha,* a general term used for openwork fabrics, were woven there. [155] An English language China coast journal of 1835 tells us that this office was under a special minister and eight subordinates but, as yet, no silk has been found in any western collection which bears the mark of this official or the establishment under his charge.

Lengths of fabric, whether woven in Peking or elsewhere, were stored there in one of the imperial depositories and requisitioned when required. There seem to

85

have been dressmakers as well as embroiderers employed within the palace although arrangements were sometimes made for the embroidery work to be executed in the city of Suzhou. [156] The Board of Rites laid down designs for robes each year. With reference to the court robe belonging to the Qianlong emperor and mentioned above (p. 29) it has been calculated from Qing archival sources that it would have taken one person sixteen days to accomplish the pattern drawing, one year and one month to complete the gold work and one year and four months for the silk embroidery. This excludes the time taken to weave the ground fabric. We do not know how many people worked on a piece of embroidery of this kind at any one time, but the statistics do attest to the exacting nature of the work. [157] We know too that poor commercial imitations of palace embroidery were made, indicating that a high standard of work was expected for imperial pieces, at least in the eighteenth century. [158]

Operating concurrently with the workshops in Peking but outlasting them by some fifty years were the much larger imperial silkworks, *Zhi zao ju,* 'Weaving Office', situated in and around three cities of the lower Yangtze valley, Suzhou, Hangzhou and Nanjing, some 550 miles from the capital. An investigation carried out in 1957 showed that the site of the Suzhou works, by then part of a school, covered about ten acres. It is believed that one of the buildings in the compound was used as a temporary residence or travel palace by both the Kangxi and the Qianlong emperors while making their southern tours. [159] Several dated stone monuments record various rebuilding programmes and the evidence of one erected in 1906 suggests that women were working there by that time, with the implication that until the beginning of the twentieth century the large weaving organisations were dominated by a male work force. [160]

The three official silkworks, an inheritance from the previous dynasty, supplied the Qing court with many kinds of textiles, only some of which were destined for imperial apparel. Although seven thousand wage-earning workers serviced these imperial factories at the height of the Qing dynasty in the second half of the eighteenth century, private weaving workshops were also contracted to carry out government work either by supplying skilled weavers for the government establishments or by completing orders on their own premises. Work contracted out in these ways was not just the simplest or least specialized kind. For instance, special court robes were supplied by selected private weavers. These outside commissions were not always fulfilled and even the weaving establishments directly under imperial control sometimes could not finish an order in the time allotted. [161] The *Peking Gazette* of 1890 reported the director of the imperial silk factory at Nanjing asking for an extension of time to complete robes and rolls of satin and gauze for the emperor to use as presents. [162]

By the time of this newspaper article the imperial silkworks were nearing their end, with only four more fully-operating years ahead of them. The Commission of enquiry into silk, whose findings were published in 1881, found the number of workers employed in the three official factories much reduced since the eighteenth century. Carried out by the European-staffed Imperial Maritime Customs, the survey was concerned with the entire Chinese silk industry. However, where imperial textiles are specifically singled out the wording of the report seems to suggest that by the late nineteenth century their production had become erratic and variable. F. Kleinwächter, the Commissioner of Customs based in the Nanjing area, implies that some of the dress silks produced on the official looms were made available to anyone who could afford them. Of *weituo jin*, a kind of damask interwoven with gold thread – *weituo* being the name of the Buddhist saint Vimilakirti and *jin* meaning gold – he says 'it is made almost exclusively for the Emperor, and very little is consumed by the people.' The word 'almost' invalidates it as a textile restricted to imperial use. Another commissioner, James Hart, reporting on the Suzhou and Hangzhou imperial workshops tells us that the workers there were allowed:

> 'after the completion of orders from Peking, to employ their spare time in executing private orders; but they must at all times hold themselves at the disposal of the officials. It happens occasionally that orders from the court have to be executed without delay, and weavers work night and day. There is no regular quantity produced and no-one but the official appointed to superintend that special work knows the number of pieces manufactured.'

The far-reaching investigations of these Maritime Customs Commissioners, many of whom sent information additional to that originally asked for by the Inspector General, reveal other sources of supply for the court in Peking. Chengdu and Baxian in Sichuan province supplied 'a certain quantity of silk materials' and 'a small quantity of satin' respectively while Zhangzhou near Xiamen (Amoy) manufactured velvet, all of them for imperial use. [163] Fabric from Luzhou in Shanxi province, an area of north-central China not usually associated with silk production, was used at some of the court functions up until 1884 at least, although no date is given for the start of this manufacture. [164]

We do not know today whether any of these special silks were used for dress but it seems clear that the supply of luxury textiles for the imperial household drew on the products of workshops more widely distributed than has hitherto been assumed. These workers presumably produced particularly fine or rare types of fabric not available from the larger establishments of Suzhou, Hangzhou and Nanjing. However just as no surviving garment in the Victoria and Albert Museum's collection, or indeed in any other collection outside China, can be assigned to a particular emperor, neither can any of them convincingly be attributed to any single workshop, whether in the Yangtze valley or elsewhere.

Tailoring and Garment Production

Most of the robes we have been discussing are hand-tailored with small stitches in a silk sewing thread of the same colour as the garment. Where it is possible to see the thread clearly, it is found to be an organzine, that is, a yarn formed by twisting together already twisted yarns, so making it suitably strong for dressmaking. [165]

Sewing thread appears as one of the products of Suzhou in the Customs report of 1881 where it is listed as being available in thirty-five colours. [166] It must have been produced in many other places, too.

Robes could be purchased ready-made, and there are indications of a thriving second-hand trade as well. [167] Professional tailors were also employed to make up ready-embroidered bolts of cloth. Ningbo in Zhejiang province was famous for supplying workers for the tailoring trade. According to one Chinese commentator, writing in 1838, most of the tailors in Peking came from Ningbo. [168] Sometimes they worked in their own establishments but often they took the tools of their trade to private houses. Mrs Roe, an Englishwoman resident in China at the beginning of the twentieth century, remembers such a tailor completing a Chinese lady's garment in three days. He charged fivepence a day and provided his own food. He chalked the lines of the pattern pieces onto the table and then laid the cloth in these divisions. [169] Rudolf Hommel, an American who made a first-hand study of Chinese tools in the 1920s, on the other hand, observed tailors marking the silk. Both these writers describe in detail a tailor's line marker. Ochre powder was piled on a small piece of cloth and a string laid through the middle. The ends and sides of the cloth were sewn firmly together making a parcel of the powder, with the string protruding from either end of the cloth package. 'When a line is to be marked the string is pulled through the ocher bag, held stretched over the cloth, taken in the middle, pulled up, and released, when the string thus twanged will deposit a line of the ocher dust upon the cloth.'[170]

Mrs Roe's tailor had a paste-pot as part of his equipment. As she does not tell us how he used it we can only speculate that perhaps he applied glue to the cut edges of the silk to prevent them from fraying. Seams visible on the inside of some garments reveal bindings of brown paper pasted to the raw edges. The Museum of Mankind in London has, amongst its collection of tools acquired in 1896, a paddle-shaped implement which is recorded as being a paste knife used in fixing trimming before it is sewn on. [171]

A needle with a round eye was used for sewing in China, and was helped on its way by a Chinese thimble, a simple metal band worn round the second joint of the middle finger. The completed seams were smoothed out with an iron, the fabric allowance on the inside being opened out either side of the central seams, while the inside edges of the side seams were both flattened the same way towards the back of the garment. The iron was in the form of a flat-bottomed bowl containing charcoal with a handle attachment. They seemed to have been tailors' accoutrements rather than domestic appliances, it being unusual to iron out creases from clothes once they had left the tailor's hands. [172] Lady Hosie thought the neatness of Chinese sewing was due to the fact that running stitch was not used, rather each half-stitch was made separately. [173]

Tailors would also have made up embroidered robes of gauze weave, the perforated nature of the silk making the stitching process more difficult than on silks of compact weave like the satin and twill robes described above. The blue velvet robe would have been cut and tailored from a continuous length of patterned

86 pile silk. An unmade-up bolt of black velvet has the shaped garment pieces woven into the length of the cloth. The pile has been skilfully cut so as to delineate the edges of the robe, and the borders and collars are also included. The tailor would cut around the pre-woven shapes and sew them together.

87
88 Other garments decorated as weaving progressed would also be woven to shape, with unpatterned sections of plain weave silk filling in the rest of the loom width. A lotus decorated robe for a woman in silk tapestry technique would have been woven in this way. The cuffs and edgings are similar to the main body of the garment in technique and patterning, except that their background colour is black instead of mauve. It may be that these contrasting borders were woven into the fill-in cloth at the side of the main garment shape. In any case, the collar band was woven ready curved to fit the neck opening and side closure.

Silk for robes of this complexity would have been produced in professional workshops. It is interesting that silk tapestry, despite being one of China's great contributions to weaving technology, is not often mentioned by name in any of the European or Chinese sources studied so far. Other kinds of named robe silk can be matched up, albeit imprecisely, with surviving garments, although there are numerous recorded types of silk of which the Museum has no examples. Crepe is one of these, its use on Museum pieces being confined to items made in China for export to Europe and America. It is known that there was a sizable output of crepe specifically for domestic-market clothing but no Chinese garment in the collection is made from this kind of silk. [174]

None of the made-up Chinese garments in the Museum give any indication as to their place of manufacture. Although Suzhou seems to have produced the widest variety and largest quantity of silk for clothing, the Customs Commissioners sending in returns from other centres throughout China in 1881 indicated that dress silk production was widespread. The weaver and sericulturist were not necessarily the same person, although those who carried out weaving as a slack-season activity between farming work may sometimes have reared and reeled the silk cocoons themselves. We know that at least in Suzhou and Nanjing, there were also wage-earning full-time weavers who were employed at hiring fairs and taken on according to their skills, the weaver's trade being broken down into fairly narrow specializations. There were also self-employed weavers and 'putting-out' weavers, the latter being supplied with raw materials by rich businessmen. Sometimes these men bought up the finished silk textiles themselves, sometimes a *chou ling tou* or 'silk cloth broker' acted as a middleman between the small producer and commercial buyer. [175]

Embroidery

89 If the silk for a garment was not patterned on the loom, lengths of plain, twill, satin or gauze weave cloth could be seamed together for embroidery (p. 20). The large quantity of Chinese embroidery in the Victoria and Albert Museum alone speaks of

already said.

86 *Part of a length of black silk velvet*, early 20th century, entire length 424 × 66.5 cm, T.278-1910.

On the following pages:
87 *Manchu woman's robe*, silk tapestry weave, 19th century, 140 × 205 cm, T.233-1948.

88 *Detail of 87.*

101

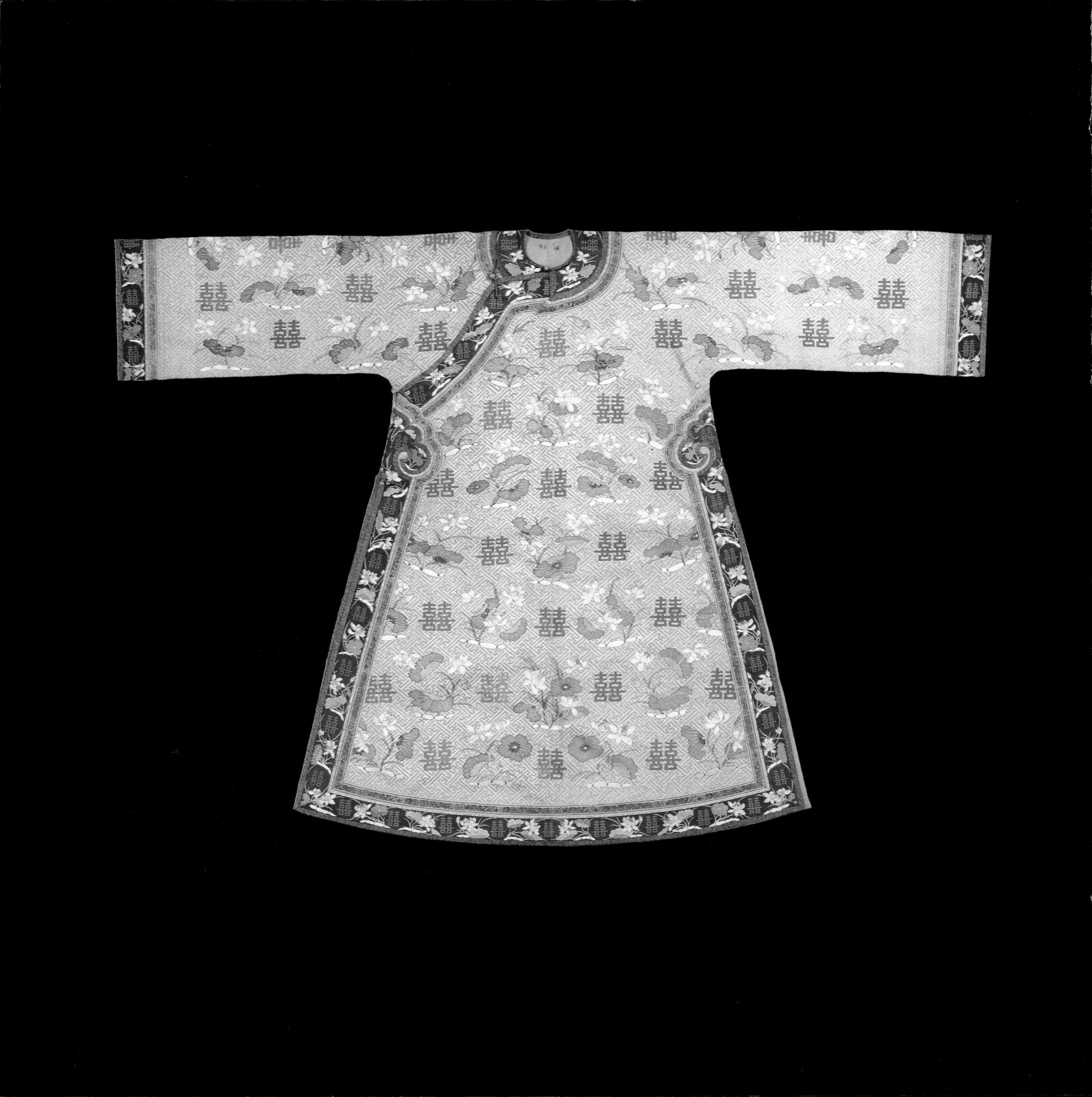

Top:
89 *Detail of robe*, embroidery on orange twill weave silk, 19th century, T.10-1967.

Bottom:
90 *Detail of 89*, showing fish scales.

Opposite:
91 *Woman embroidering*, watercolour on paper, c.1790, 35 × 42 cm, D.66-1898.

a vast number of embroidery establishments and all the European travellers whose remarks we have noted so far observed embroidered articles being made or for sale all over China. Just as for weaving, embroidery workshops must have varied greatly in size and organization. At the end of the eighteenth century, Shen Fu's future wife Yun took in embroidery work to pay her brother's tuition fees. [176] A century later, Lucy Soothill recorded how Chinese women and girls were, in some measure, able to relieve their families' poverty by working at embroidery. [177]

Mrs Soothill's women, burdened with economic insecurity, would not have borne any resemblance to the well-dressed lady portrayed in a Museum watercolour who is elegantly working on a decorative roundel. Although the social setting may be incorrect, the technical details showing the silk stretched on a bamboo frame give us an accurate picture of the methods professional workers used to embroider large pieces of cloth. While this embroiderer has all the appearances of a lady of leisure, it is doubtful whether such women would have regularly set up large frames; domestic embroidery was probably confined to small articles. Supplementary information, in the form of a handwritten key accompanying the set of watercolours of which this is one, tells us 'this business is generally performed by men but in the same manner'. Several observers, presumably surprised at finding a situation different from that in the Europe they knew, remarked on the

105

male labour force of the Chinese embroidery trade. We know, however, that in 1881 there were 1,050 working people in Suzhou engaged in embroidery work and that these were principally women and young girls. [178]

European visitors of both sexes saw large embroideries such as banners, furnishings and robes throughout China, but it was only the lady travellers who were able to observe, by virtue of their being women, the Chinese domestic scene where the smaller items of handwork were made. Although they did not lead such restricted lives as their Chinese counterparts, the unenlightened boundaries of the Victorian and Edwardian European lady visitor's position often limited her observations to sentimental admiration, overlooking the fact that there was no choice for Chinese women: all women of the leisured classes had to spend time embroidering. The ill-rendered stitches on some small embroideries would seem to bear this out, for in the non-professional sphere the range of accomplishment was very wide.

In *The Story of the Stone* all the young women and their maids embroider. The maxim 'a girl's first concern is to be virtuous, her second industrious' is reiterated in different forms throughout the novel. It was needlework that provided the outward sign of industry and it was always to take precedence over book learning. Grandmother Jia, the family matriarch, has no objection to girls learning their letters but needlework has to come first. Interestingly, she says, 'in a family like ours we never need to do our own sewing, I know. But it's as well to know how. Then you will never need to be at the mercy of others'. [179] She presumably was not envisaging them ever having to earn a living, rather being able to keep up appearances and standards should hard times strike.

The idea of the devil making work for idle hands held true for Chinese women, as it did for generations of western women. One English sampler gives us a rare glimpse of the frustration that must have been felt by many who were forced by the mores of their society, whether Chinese or western, to embroider subserviently. Worked by a young girl the stitches form the words, 'Polly Cook did it and she hated every stitch she did in it'. [180]

Chinese embroidery, while employing many stitches familiar in the West, has its own distinctive techniques. As we have seen, the background material for Chinese embroidered garments can be plain, twill, or satin weave silk, simple gauze weave silk, silk with gauze weave decoration against a plain weave ground, velvet, and (to a lesser extent) self-patterned silk. This last fabric is more often left completely unadorned when used for men's garments, while for women's garments it is decorated with embroidered collar bands and cuffs only. Apart from dragon robes it was unusual for Chinese men to wear embroidered clothes at all, roundel patterns, butterflies, floral and fruiting sprays, and garden vignettes being reserved for women. Pattern books of these designs must have been readily available and widely utilized although very few have survived to the present time. Woodblocks were used to print the pattern in black outline onto thin paper sheets which were then made up into books. It is not altogether clear how the pattern was then transferred to the fabric but the scarcity of extant pattern books suggests that the paper pages may have been used up in either tracing or pouncing the design through onto the cloth. It would have needed a skilled worker to copy the designs freehand, but this may well have been the method in the professional workshops where someone was probably employed especially for this task leaving others to carry out the actual embroidery. Outworkers also seem to have made a living this way. In 1887 Edwin Dukes, an English missionary in China, recorded seeing a man:

> 'producing a truly admirable piece of work. Seated on a low stool, he has placed on his knees a board upon which is spread a piece of fine linen, and, undisturbed by the busy traffic, he is drawing with a camel's-hair pencil dipped in Indian ink patterns to be sold to persons skilled in working with coloured silks... He uses neither rule nor compass, yet every stroke is produced with mathematical accuracy. Some of the finished pieces are covered with flowers and wreaths, and birds, and human figures portrayed with a delicacy of touch which would do credit to a first-rate lithographic artist. It is true he only attempts a regular round of patterns, and that he has done each of them hundreds of times; but still the work is done, and with the perfection that you see'. [181]

In the case of most painted silks produced in China but destined for export to Europe and America, the outline design was first printed straight onto the textile, and then filled in with colours applied by hand with a brush. [182] It may well be that in some instances a printed outline was also used as a guide for embroiderers, but as yet it has not been possible to verify this. On small items the embroidery was sometimes executed straight onto the silk without the aid of any sort of pattern. Where a piece is unfinished, where the embroidery silk has rotted away, or where the stitches have not quite covered the outline it is sometimes possible, with magnification, to detect the original guidelines. This is seen either as a thin black ink line, or as a wider, white chalky line fixed with a clear adhesive. The former would suggest any of the modes of application put forward above with the exception of pouncing. The white line may indicate this technique, whereby powder is systematically released from a small muslin bag along the already pricked lines of a paper design laid on top of the fabric. To prevent the transferred powder line from smudging or disappearing before the embroidery was completed it was painted with glue as a fixative.

The central seams would be sewn together at the back and front of a Chinese garment before the design was marked out. In this way, when the embroidery came to be executed across the joins it would match without a break in the middle. Large items to be embroidered would be stretched across wooden frames often with a worker sitting on either side, each one manipulating the needle and thread with both hands, one hand above the cloth, the other beneath. With very few exceptions the embroidery silk used was untwisted giving a sheen to the finished work. In modern times Chinese embroiderers have developed a way of dividing this floss silk into near-invisible hair-like strands but this was not the practice in the eighteenth, nineteenth and early twentieth centuries. Apart from the inherent glossiness of the thread, the lustre characteristic of Chinese embroideries was achieved by the use of straight parallel stitches laid side by side. On the best worked pieces the angle of the satin stitch, as this technique is called, was often altered from motif to motif, resulting in a different play of light reflected from the surface.

We can gain some idea of embroidery methods by studying unlined clothes and sleevebands where the backs of the stitches are visible, bearing in mind that this may not give us a true overall picture, as the majority of garments are lined. However, where it is possible to see the reverse, the satin stitch is found to pass across both back and front of the fabric in most cases. There are only a few verifiable examples in the Museum's collection showing surface satin stitch. This version of the stitch floats across the front surface of the fabric only. On the back are short horizontal stitches following the outline of the motif. It is harder to achieve a neat line with this method, and it is less suitable for the Chinese practice of encroaching one line of stitches up into the next of a paler or darker shade of the same colour. With double-faced satin stitch the embroiderer can so arrange the order of working the lines that the needle always comes up from the back at a point where the ground fabric is free from other stitches. With surface satin stitch this is not the case. The difficulty of bringing the needle up between two already tight-packed stitches, and the risk of the floss silk fluffing as it rubs past them, limits the use of surface stitching on this type of shaded embroidery. The double-faced satin stitch does not make for reversible clothes. There is no attempt, as there is for example on banners, to make the back as neat as the front. As another precaution against fluffing, fairly short lengths of thread are used resulting in a lot of cut or tucked-in ends on the back.

In defining the satin stitch variations, we have mentioned two very common characteristics of Chinese embroidery, encroaching and shading. The two generally go together. The encroaching stitch, whereby each new stitch fits in between the base of the two on the row before, can look like long and short stitch to the naked eye, and has been identified as such by a number of writers. For the most part, long and short stitch is not found on items of Chinese dress although it may prove to be more commonly used on furnishings and hangings. Because the strands of floss silk tend to separate out in the middle of each stitch and come together again where they go through the fabric, this gives the false impression of two stitches, a long one and a short one, laid down side by side.

Where one motif or section of a motif ends and the next one begins, Chinese embroiderers leave a thin line of the ground material free from stitching. This voiding, as it is called, gives a sculptural effect to the work and makes clear the boundary lines where satin stitch predominates. [183] Examples of voiding can be found in many of the illustrations to this volume. A line of yellow ground silk can be seen around the red bat at the bottom of the detail of the dragon robe hem illustrated. Despite the enviable precision of this kind of satin stitch work, typical of the mid- and late-Qing, it has a certain mechanical look. When put beside early eighteenth century embroidery it suffers by comparison. The early examples, while they may not be as neatly executed, utilize both the shading and voiding techniques with greater imagination. Where there is no shading, as on the blue overall fret shown here, the length of each satin stitch is adjusted to fill the design.

In a more innovative vein, long floss stitches secured only at their ends can be laid

down side by side to cover a required shape. Finer threads of a contrasting colour are then floated across these in an open geometric pattern perhaps in the form of scales, plumage, or a trellis design. The long floss stitches may be secured or couched down by these trellis threads going through the ground, or the trellis threads themselves may be fixed down along with the original long stitches by small stitches sewn across both. The cracked ice pattern on the white vase on the
39 green skirt is an example of this three-part laid and couched method. The fish scales
90 on a lady's red robe are another variation. A complicated lace-like pattern with no underlying floss floats is seen on one of the fan cases. This is what the Chinese call
59 *wang xiu,* 'net embroidery'. It is a monochromatic interlace filling. Such highly decorative techniques are used sparingly on Chinese dress, providing spots of relief between the bands of satin stitch. The pale green robe decorated with many of these complex stitch arrangements was originally meant for a hanging as we have seen (p. 61) and this style of embroidery is more often found on furnishings.

Other flat stitches used in Chinese dress embroidery are those which radiate from
93 a central hole to form flower stamens or stylized pine needles. Stem stitch is used for
92 veining leaves and for the manes and tails of dragons and other beasts. It is regularly worked in close curving lines to form the rounded tops of the waves on the striped hem decoration.

The waves, like many of the standard motifs found on decorated Chinese garments, are sometimes enhanced with gold work. This never seems to be pure gold, but there is always some gold present along with iron, lead, copper and sometimes silver. At the present time some doubt exists as to the form of the elements found and only further tests will verify whether they are alloyed or surface coated. The metal seems to be backed onto paper and then spiralled round a silk thread core. Here are John Henry Gray's observations of the process:

'Sheets of paper are coated in earth or glue and covered with gold and silver leaf. To bring out the glossiness the sheets are rubbed with chrystals *[sic]* on the end of bamboo sticks. The sheets are then cut with large knives into strips and wound round ordinary silk threads'. [184]

Although the colour of the metal thread varies from silvery to shiny red and yellow, the metallic make-up does not seem to alter significantly. This stiff thread cannot be pulled through the background silk in the normal way but must be laid on the surface and anchored by small couching stitches which are often yellow to blend in with the gold but are sometimes found in other colours. Gold-wrapped threads are used singly when outlining small design elements. They are couched down two at a time, often with three pairs alongside each other, to form garment borders. Metallic thread is also shaped into scales, flowers, insects and landscape elements.
94 For this each thread or pair of threads is twisted into the desired shape and pressed into place with a hot iron before being couched down. [185] In the case of theatre costume the gold is raised up over some form of padding. As well as gold-wrapped thread, white twisted silk is used for couched outlines. This is usually a spiral thread with one strand wound tightly or loosely round another which may be of equal
95 thickness to the first, or may be finer to produce a more knotty appearance.

On the following pages:
92 *Detail of robe*, embroidery on satin weave silk, 19th century, T. 12-1950.

93 *Detail of 32.*

Below:
94 *Detail of robe*, showing laid and couched work in gold-wrapped thread, T. 197-1948.

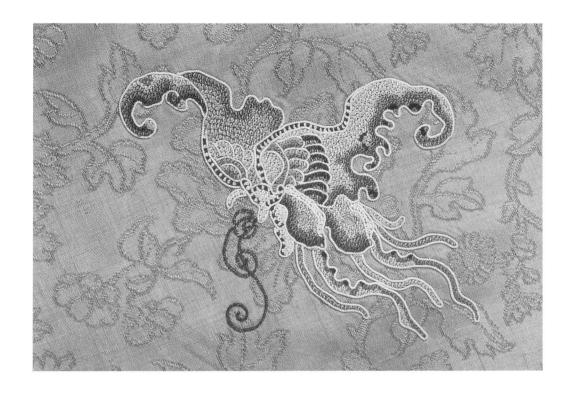

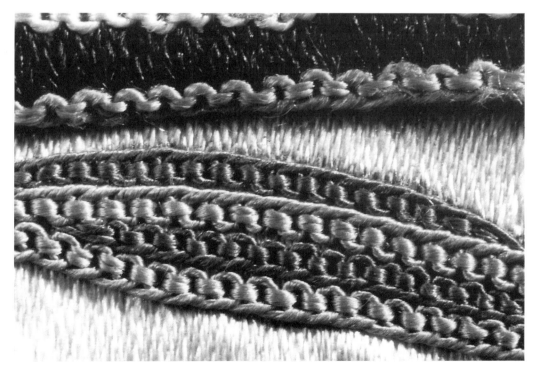

Top:
95 *Detail of robe*, embroidery on blue plain weave silk with gauze weave decoration, late 19th century, T. 53-1970.

Bottom:
96 *Detail of 58*.

112

Couched twisted silk in other colours is sometimes used as infilling.

Another kind of stitch which was increasingly used to fill design shapes, but which in the eighteenth and early part of the nineteenth centuries had been used only for highlighting was the seed stitch (da zi 'making seeds'). This is not the seed stitch used in Europe for speckling. It is similar though not identical to the French
92 knot. It is sometimes pulled tightly to produce neat flower centres and sometimes
95 worked loosely, forming a ring-like stitch more suitable for covering larger areas. Like gold work, seed stitch is more effectively used in combination with other embroidery techniques. A modern Chinese embroidery manual places seed stitch in a category called rao xiu, rao meaning 'to go around' and xiu meaning 'embroidery'. Another stitch which according to the Chinese belongs in this group
96 is formed from rows of tiny loops secured down with back stitch. Its execution is minute and even. It is done with two needles, the loops and the backstitches attaching them to the ground being worked all in one journey. The European method is to make two journeys, the first one to make a line of backstitch and the second to loop a thread, sometimes in a different colour, through this line. This is commonly called 'Pekinese stitch' in the West, but the name is not known in China. The Chinese term is la suozi (literally to 'shoot the bolt across') or da daozi (literally to 'strike upside down'). It does not seem to be of any antiquity and is most frequently used on accessories. [186]

In the Qing dynasty (1644-1911), counted thread work was practised in two ways. Both give a formality to the finished work, the stitches being passed over a set number of ground fabric threads. The open grid of gauze weave would seem to lend itself to this technique. In the first of the methods, vertical or slanted stitches are passed across the fabric in regular formation. Sometimes the stitches completely cover the ground weave and sometimes only selected areas are decorated. We have already noted a gauze weave court robe belonging to the Qianlong emperor embroidered in this way (p. 29). The Museum's examples of counted thread work date from a later period than this and on many of these the generally supple nature of the silk gauze has resulted in distorted work. Sometimes the Chinese gauze is of an equal stiffness to the canvas used in Europe for the same purpose. [187] The greater rigidity of the ground makes for stitches of an absolute regularity, a prerequisite for good counted thread work. This is well illustrated by the central lotus design on the
65 Museum's doudou worked on stiffened gauze.

This same piece gives us an example of the second type of counted thread work. The interlocking effect of the blue fret background framing the flowers is achieved by taking the embroidery silk around the horizontal weft threads of the ground in an ordered sequence. The stitches run in the same direction as the warp threads, entirely covering them. Each block of glossy blue stitches is worked in one go. The horizontal stitches of European pattern darning, by contrast, run across the entire width of the ground which in part remains visible. [188] The ground in the Chinese version is completely hidden. The geometric pattern is in fact formed out of the spaces in the embroidery where one block ends and the next begins.

Finally, although it is not truly an embroidery technique, appliqué should be mentioned here as another way of embellishing Chinese dress and accessories. One of the fan cases illustrated earlier has this decoration. The flowers are cut out of different coloured silks, their edges are turned under and they are sewn onto the black background with matching thread. Another form of appliqué seen at the jacket corners of the purple trouser suit and used this way on early twentieth century women's garments is formed by cutting out a shaped section of the top layer of silk to reveal a contrasting coloured silk beneath. In this case it is the blue satin embroidered edging that has been decoratively cut, and a patch of pale lilac silk has been secured beneath this cut-out shape. The edges of the cut blue satin have been bound with black and stitched down. [189]

59

40

A Note on Dating

No aspect of the study of Chinese dress presents greater problems than that of dating. Books published in China are often more non-committal about this than those written by western scholars and most Chinese writers prefer to allow a wide margin of error, consigning garments to the Qing dynasty (1644-1911) without any further refinement. Several attempts at more precise periodization have been made in conjunction with exhibitions of Chinese dress from North American collections. [190] These have produced some intelligent theses in this difficult field and our knowledge would be poorer without them. However, their dating is based mainly on two factors which, while not totally invalid, must now be held in question. The first involves the study of twelve symbol robes, their assignment to certain emperors, their consequent dating, and by inference the dating of other robes. We have already seen that it is rarely possible to prove imperial ownership of robes now in western collections (p. 36). The second uses the design arrangement as a guide to dating, but it only concerns itself with dragon robes. The form of the striped water pattern at the hem, the height of the mountain motif rising from the waves and the style of the cloud formations, all supposedly indicative of a certain time of manufacture, cannot be used as sure dating criteria. We know that during the Qing dynasty garments were regularly made in what were believed to be earlier styles. [191] In addition there is evidence that dragon robes with different styles were worn at the same period. [192] A beautifully-worked pale orange dragon robe in the Museum illustrates some of the obstacles to the development of a sure system for dating Chinese dress. It has the wispy five-colour clouds and the undulating water pattern thought by some writers to date from the eighteenth century. The slender mountain form which, in this questionable dating scheme, should also appear is here absent and its design is not particularly attenuated. The garment itself is elegantly tailored, the side seams gradually sloping outwards from top to bottom, a graceful, fitted shape which may also indicate an eighteenth century date. Although many quite obviously late nineteenth and twentieth century examples are not at all shaped this element alone does not provide a watertight dating criterion. One certain observation we can make about this orange satin robe is that the neckband and horsehoof cuffs are embroidered in the same way as many other dragon robes whereas the work on the rest of the garment is less familiar. Moving into the realms of considered guesswork, we can perhaps say that the cuffs and neckband may have been added later along with the incongruous yellow lower sleeves. When all the evidence, however speculative, is brought together the robe can be placed somewhere between the last decade of the eighteenth century and the middle years of the nineteenth, a period we shall call 'mid Qing'.

97

With a very few exceptions, it has only been possible to date the Museum's collection within broad time spans. Even then there has been uncertainty about which span some garments belong to. The periods themselves must also remain loosely defined as to the exact years of their beginning. We have looked at the process, albeit fallible, of dating a robe to the mid Qing period. Next we will attempt to demonstate why a red embroidered robe may be 'early Qing', the time

98
99 span covering the late seventeenth century and most of the eighteenth. It may also be the earliest secular garment for a woman in the Museum's collection. It is small compared with many other similarly-cut coats. Made from a rich red silk it unusually has horizontal bands of fruiting pomegranates in gauze weave running across the fabric at widely-spaced intervals. The design is embroidered in very soft floss silk and gold-wrapped thread which proves to have much the same make up as that on other robes in the Museum (p. 109). The 'phoenix' with streamer-like tail at the top centre, the flying cranes below waist level, and the waves and tall triple mountain at the hem all appear with variations of colouring on the front. The green and white hydrangea flowers on both sleeve backs are replaced by a pomegranate and peach on the sleeve fronts, and the cranes curled up in peaches below the 'phoenix' do not appear on the other side. The gold scaly creatures with hoofs near the bottom are matched on the front by a pair of leonine beasts with paws and curly manes. The floral branches meander across the silk's surface in an open, free design, one of them changing into a dragon as it emerges from behind the crane roundel to the right. The white gauze cuffs embroidered with pairs of fishes and flowers, the ribbon trimming and the blue and white embroidered edging on black are all probably later than the main garment, as is the blue lining. The quality of the red silk with its gauze inserts, the arrangement of the design and the embroidery technique make it unusual within the Museum's collection and mark it as different from those embroideries, here exemplified by the cuffs, which can with some confidence be dated to the nineteenth century. The striped hem decoration found on so many Chinese garments is here absent and the design is balanced though not symmetrical. The flowers themselves are not easy to recognise botanically as they all share the same foliage, a feature also found on the Spanish cope made from Chinese embroidery and now in the Malmö Museum in Sweden. Although justification for a seventeenth century date for his church vestment is tenuous the work seems very similar to the piece illustrated here. [193] More firmly datable is a hanging, also in Sweden, in the Museum of Far Eastern Antiquities in Stockholm. A dedicatory inscription and the date 1705 were added to this unquestionably Chinese embroidered velvet which bears similar animals to the ones at the hem of the Victoria and Albert Museum's garment. [194]

Satin stitches, the small knot known as seed stitch for flower centres and birds' heads, and gold couching are the principle embroidery techniques employed on this piece. In this respect it does not differ from the bulk of Chinese embroidery. However, the satin stitch is not consistently packed tightly together as it is on the cuffs, and the use of voiding is more intuitive (p. 108). The edge of each individual motif is finished predominantly in white, another unusual feature. The later cuffs

116

are proof that this robe was lovingly preserved, and that its pleasing design and colours, together with the quality of the work, offset any awkwardness the wearer might have felt about it being unfashionable in the nineteenth century. It may have been kept for special occasions.

This justification for a particular date is neither possible nor desirable for most of the collection. We should view with caution any too precise dating of a garment. Certainly it is important and exciting to be able to place an object in its correct historical setting, and for that reason we should sometimes work towards more exact dating. However, as has been demonstrated there are many ways of looking at Chinese dress. The date may not necessarily be the most crucial fact.

We should mention several robes, or rather parts of robes, which although very different in style from the red robe discussed above, may belong to the same period. One of them may even pre-date the Qing dynasty. All of them fall into the general category of robes with lobed collar designs. They are similar to the top part of a court robe, although the dragons loop over the shoulders, and resemble examples in the Palace Museum, Peking which have been published with a Ming dynasty date (1368-1644). [195] Portraits of the Ming élite do show them wearing such robes. These two references would seem to provide obvious sources for a framework of

100 *Buddhist priest's mantle*, made up in Japan from Chinese brocaded silk of the first half of the 17th century, 113 × 214 cm, T.138-1927.

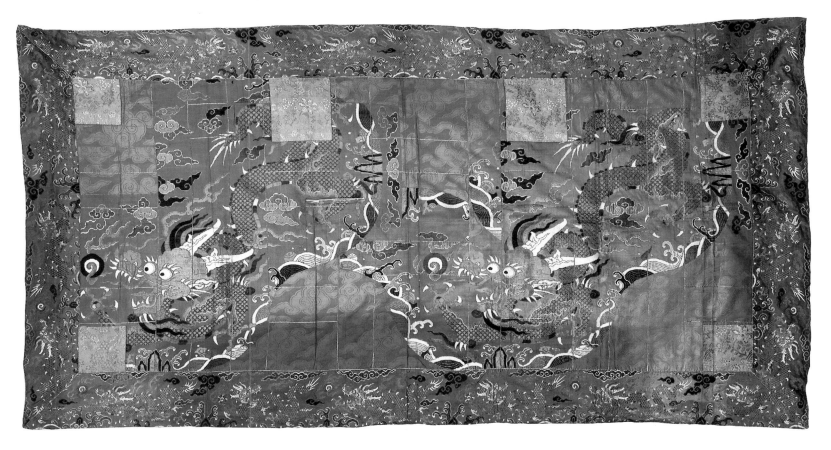

dating and it may seem surprising that neither inventoried garments nor paintings have yet been cited specifically for this purpose. Both of them are of value but there are pitfalls involved here too. While we know that there are many hundreds of robes in the Palace Museum in Peking (Note 58) and while some of them appear to be labelled or inventoried, we also learn from an eminent Chinese scholar that this information is not necessarily always accurate. [196]

Painting in the high Chinese tradition is of very little use for dating garments. Precision of record was of no concern to most élite artists; it was actually avoided for its association with the socially less-acceptable skills of the artisan painter. The products of the latter's workshops, however, in the form of commissioned portraits and often rigorously-observed records of court ceremonial, do retain a certain value for the historian of dress. Before using any painting as the basis for an argument on the dating of Chinese applied arts we must first ascertain its position in the broad spectrum of traditional styles of pictorial representation.

The justification for a pre-Qing date for sections of red Chinese robe silk now
100 made up into a Japanese Buddhist priest's mantle partly rests on the evidence of portrait paintings in which sixteenth and seventeenth century officials are seen to be wearing red robes, the acknowledged colour for official garments of the Ming dynasty. [197] During the Qing dynasty (1644-1911) red remained a festive occasion colour, and was worn by women and actors. It was not worn by anyone in an official capacity except at the annual ritual court ceremony at the Altar of the Sun (p. 33). The red colour and the looping dragons on the Victoria and Albert Museum's mantle make it unlikely that the material was originally intended for a Qing court robe. Thus it can be given a Ming dynasty date, in the first half of the seventeenth century. [198]

Articles of clothing excavated from dated Chinese tombs are mostly too early to have any bearing on the dating of the Museum's collection. When robes are not merely called 'Qing', Chinese writers tend to assign them to the various emperors' reigns, as is traditional with porcelain. [199] While they do not always give their reasons for this dating, western researchers must respect the knowledge implied. It has always been thought that, because of the colours, design and quality, the man's blue court skirt mentioned earlier (p. 33) must be from the eighteenth century. This dating has been further confirmed by the publication of a woman's sleeveless coat from the Palace Museum, Peking resembling the skirt in several respects, and dated by the Chinese to the Yongzheng emperor's reign (r. 1723-1735). [200]

Palace Museum objects with exact dates are rare, but several embroidered roundels from ladies' robes have been so designated, presumably because they are labelled in some undisclosed way. They guide us when trying to put a date on some of the Museum's women's clothes, since these have a very similar design
101 arrangement and execution to the published examples. Plate 101 has a counterpart in China which is dated to 1759, a surprisingly early date. [201]

So far we have been able to show that some Chinese dress can be dated within the broad periods of 'early' and 'mid Qing'. The bright purple colour on many Chinese garments is not found on those from these first two periods. Although a scientific

Opposite:
97 *Dragon robe*, embroidery on satin weave silk, late 18th – middle of the 19th century (mid-Qing), 138.5 × 189 cm, T. 108-1967.

118

Top left:
101 *Detail of robe*, embroidery on blue gauze
    weave silk, c.1759, T.32-1950.

Top right:
102 *Detail of robe*, embroidery on blue plain
    weave silk weave, c.1865, T.162-1969.

120

analysis has not yet been concluded within the Museum, this intense purple colour is acknowledged to be an aniline dye, one of the early synthetics. The first synthetic dyes were invented in Europe around the mid-nineteenth century and continued to be developed thereafter. [202] A Chinese embroidered hanging (T.266-1960) with a date equivalent to 1871 painted onto the silk manifestly contains this purple dye, providing a pointer as to the time of its introduction into China. Methyl Violet 2B, the aniline dye identified on one Chinese garment, was not produced in quantity until 1866, and research carried out on customs returns proves the importation of aniline dyes into China in 1871. [203] So although we do not know exactly when aniline dyes first appeared on Chinese textiles, we can confidently say that garments containing them must belong to the time span we shall call 'late Qing', covering the last three decades of the nineteenth century and the beginning of the twentieth. We have seen that traditional clothes were made right up to and in some cases beyond the 1949 Revolution, and although we can sometimes distinguish those made in the 1920s and 1930s from those made before the fall of the Qing dynasty in 1911 this is not always the case. [204] For this reason an even longer time span is sometimes applied and as this period extends beyond late Qing times it has to be called an imprecise 'nineteenth or twentieth century'. We must also remember when studying these late periods that natural dyes continued to be used in the twentieth century, making the absence of aniline colouring no guarantee of an early date. One embroidery establishment in Peking which was still producing work for the imperial household at the beginning of the twentieth century was not using aniline dyed silk at that time. [205] The introduction of aniline dyes was not the only innovation of that era which, unknowingly, helps towards a dating scheme for Chinese dress. From the 1860s onwards, photography, while not revealing any great precision in the matter, enables us to trace general trends.

In attempting to date the Museum's Chinese dress we have so far referred to sources outside the Museum. Internal evidence is provided in three ways, and we shall now look at each of these in turn to see what contribution they make to the periodization of the collection. Of those image robes and ritual robes which bear inscriptions (p. 84), only one is dated to a specific year, 1830 (T.290-1962). The others bear 'cyclical' dates. This means that any one of a number of dates at sixty year intervals could apply. Because these inscribed robes bear very little resemblance to the secular dress with which we are mostly concerned they have not been found useful for dating purposes.

The second type of internal evidence is supplied by a garment which was acquired by the Museum in 1863 as 'Modern Chinese' (9148-1863). It is registered as a lady's robe, although it has a hemp lining similar to those found on image robes. Its condition is commensurate with its having been draped over a statue for some considerable time. The decoration is of a sparse dragon robe type and the embroidery is coarsely executed on red satin. Surprisingly few items of Chinese dress came into the Museum in the nineteenth century and apart from the 1863 robe none of them were recorded as being contemporary with their acquisition date.

102 A bright blue embroidered dragon robe provides us with an example of the third

On the following pages:
98 *Back of woman's robe*, embroidery on gauze-banded plain weave silk, late 17th–18th century (early Qing), 122 × 124 cm, T.184-1948.

99 *Detail of 98.*

type of internal evidence, which happily is of a more definite nature, unusual in this speculative field. The garment belonged to Thomas Lyster who was given the right to wear a dragon robe when serving in China under Charles Gordon ('Gordon of Khartoum') in the 1860s. It was donated to the Museum by one of Lyster's relatives, who also drew the Museum's attention to his book *With Gordon in China*. This records the robe's acquisition just prior to 30 March 1865. [206] The robe is in excellent condition and its unusual colouring both as regards the background material and the embroidery silks, together with the use of twisted silk embroidery thread instead of floss silk (p. 107), make it obviously different from many other dragon robes. Neither the quality of the needlework nor the general design are at all remarkable. Perhaps robes of this kind – the Museum has another near-identical one (T. 169-1970) – were made especially for foreigners in China at that time.

Notes

1 *Zhongguo pao fu zhi xiu xuan cui/Chinese Costumes, Brocade, Embroidery,* Guoli lishi bowuguan (Taibei, 1977), Shen Congwen, *Zhongguo gudai fushi yanjiu* (Researches in Ancient Chinese Dress) (Hong Kong, 1981).

2 *Yule-tide gifts,* Liberty & Co. catalogue 34 (London, 1895-1896), p.21. *Chinese Embroideries,* Debenham and Freebody catalogue (London, 1915), p.1.

3 Christopher Wood, 'Evelyn Waugh: A Pioneer Collector', *The Connoisseur,* 208 (September 1981), 30-34 (p.33).

4 Samuel Couling, *Encyclopaedia Sinica* (Shanghai, 1917), p.129.

5 Reginald F. Johnston, *Twilight in the Forbidden City* (London, 1934), p.186.

6 Lucy Soothill, *A Passport to China* (London, 1931), p.327 and p.202.

7 Clark Worswick and Jonathan Spence, *Imperial China: Photographs 1850-1912* (New York, 1978), p.73 and p.21.

8 Mrs Archibald Little, *Intimate China* (London, 1901), p.188.

9 Schuyler Cammann, 'The Development of the Mandarin Square', *Harvard Journal of Asiatic Studies,* 8 (1944), 71-130 (pp.103-110).

10 Le Père Simon Kiong, *Politesse Chinoise,* Variétés sinologiques, 25 (Shanghai, 1906), pp.26-28.

11 Shen Fu, *Six Records of a Floating Life,* translated by Leonard Pratt and Chiang Su-hui (London, 1983), p.106.

12 Lady Hosie, *Two Gentlemen of China* (London, 1924), p.243.

13 John K. Fairbank, Edwin O. Reischauer and Albert M. Craig, *East Asia: Tradition and Transformation* (Boston, 1973), p.567, *Chinese Repository,* 4 (July, 1835), p.131.

14 Lady Hosie, p.83.

15 Zhang Dechang, *Qing ji yige jing guan de shenghuo* (The life of a capital official in the late Qing) (Hong Kong, 1970), p.16.

16 *Palastmuseum Peking: Schätze aus der Verbotenen Stadt,* edited by Herbert Butz and Lothar Ledderose, Berlin Festival (Berlin, 1985), pp.159-160.

17 Schuyler Cammann, *China's Dragon Robes* (New York, 1952), pp.94-97.

18 Derek Gillman, 'Ming and Qing ivories: figure carving', in *Chinese Ivories from the Shang to the Qing,* Oriental Ceramic Society/British Museum (London, 1984), pp.35-117 (p.43).

19 Schuyler Camman, 'Notes on the origin of Chinese k'o-ssu tapestry', *Artibus Asiae,* 11(1948), 90-110.

20 Schuyler Camman, 'Origins of the court and official robes of the Ch'ing dynasty', *Artibus Asiae,* 12(1949), 189-201 (p.189).

21 Dorothy K. Burnham, *Cut My Cote,* Royal Ontario Museum (Toronto, 1973), p.33.

22 John E. Vollmer, *In the Presence of the Dragon Throne: Ch'ing Dynasty Costume (1644-1911) in the Royal Ontario Museum* (Toronto, 1977), p.21.

23 Wang Yunying, 'Huang Taiji de changfu pao' (An everyday robe of Huang Taiji), *Gugong bowuyuan yuankan* (1983.3), 91-94.

24 Walter A. Fairservis, Jr., *Costumes of the East,* The American Museum of Natural History (Riverside, 1971), p.140.

25 Manduertu, 'Cong jiating gongshe dao diyu gongshe – Oulunchun zu yuanshi shengchan fangshi de jieti' (From the household commune to the territorial commune – an analysis of a primitive mode of production of the Oroqen nationality), *Wenwu* (1976.7), 62-73 (p.71).

26 Owen Lattimore, *Studies in Frontier History: Collected Papers 1929-1958* (London, 1962), pp.370-371.

27 Henny Harald Hansen, *Mongol Costumes,* Nationalmuseets Skrifter, Etnografisk Raekke III (Copenhagen, 1950), p.xx introduction.

28 'Fuzhou shi bei jiao Nan Song mu qingli jian bao' (Report on a Southern Song tomb in the northern outskirts of Fuzhou city), *Wenwu* (1977.7), 1-16.

29 'Zouxian Yuandai Li Yu'an mu qingli jian bao' (Report on the Yuan dynasty tomb of Li Yu'an at Zouxian), *Wenwu* (1978.4), 14-18, Hansen, pp.102-103, Burnham, *Cut My Cote,* pp.29-31.

30 'Jiangxi Nancheng Ming Yixuan Wang Zhu Yijin fu fu he zang mu' (The joint tomb of Zhu Yijin, Ming Prince of Yixuan, and his wives at Nancheng, Jiangxi), *Wenwu* (1982.8), 16-28 (p.26), 'Suzhou Huqiu Wang Xijue mu qingli jilüe' (Report on the tomb of Wang Xijue at Huqiu, Suzhou), *Wenwu* (1975.3), 51-59 (p.55).

31 Camman, *China's Dragon Robes,* p.245.

32 Hansen, p.24.

33 *Ming Qing renwu xiaoxianghua xuan/Portrait Paintings of the Ming and Qing Dynasties,* Nanjing Museum (Shanghai, 1979), pls.10, 11, 12, 16 and 19.

34 Ye Mengzhu, *Yue shi bian,* Ming Qing biji congshu (Shanghai, 1981), pp.173-175.

35 Cammann, 'The Development of the Mandarin Square', p.81.

36 Cammann, 'The Development of the Mandarin Square', pp.98-99.

37 Soothill, p.260.

38 George Wingfield Digby, 'Chinese Costume in the light of an illustrated Catalogue from the Summer Palace', *Gazette des Beaux-Arts,* 41 (1953), 37-50, Margaret Medley, 'The "Illustated Regulations for Ceremonial Paraphernalia of the Ch'ing Dynasty" in the Victoria and Albert Museum', *Transactions of the Oriental Ceramic Society,* 31 (1958-1959), 95-104.

39 Kiong, p.22 and p.28.

40 Ye Mengzhu, p.177.

41 Ye Mengzhu, p.176.

42 *Report by Consul-General Hosie on the Province of Ssuch'uan,* HMSO (London, 1904), p.39.

43 Kiong, p.27.

44 Cammann, *China's Dragon Robes,* p.135.

45 Vollmer, p.39.

46 Zhang Dechang, p.117.

47 Cao Xueqin, *The Story of the Stone,* translated by David Hawkes and David Minford, 5 vols (London, 1973-11,567.

48 Chen Juanjuan, 'Qianlong yu yong chuo sha xiu xia chao pao' (An embroidered openwork gauze *chao pao* worn by the Qianlong emperor), *Gugong bowuyuan yuankan* (1984.2), 89-93 (p.89).

49 *Gugong tu xiang xuan cui/Masterpieces of Chinese Portrait Painting in the National Palace Museum* (Taipei, 1971), plate 44.

50 Ye Mengzhu, p.176.

51 *Zi jin cheng di hou shenghuo* (Lives of the Emperors and Empresses in the Forbidden City) (Peking, 1982), p.67.

52 Cammann, *China's Dragon Robes,* pp.138-139.

53 Vollmer, p.33 and p.36.

54 'Fajue Ming Zhu Tan mu jilüe' (Report on the discovery of the Ming dynasty tomb of Zhu Tan), *Wenwu* (1972.5), 25-36 (p.35).

55 'Ming Xu Da wu shi sun Xu Fu fu fu mu' (The Ming dynasty tomb of Xu Fu, fifth generation descendant of Xu Da, and his wife), *Wenwu* (1982.2), 28-32 (pl.3).

56 *Palastmuseum Peking: Schätze aus der Verbotenen Stadt,* p.8, p.57, p.122 and p.124.

57 Chen Juanjuan, p.89.

58 Shen Congwen, p.463.

59 *Gugong bowuyuan yuankan* (1980.2), colour plate 1.

60 *Zi jin cheng di hou shenghuo,* p.9, p.25 and p.71.

61 Cammann, *China's Dragon Robes,* p.71.

62 Shang Hongkui, 'Qingdai Xiaozhuang Xiaoqin liang taihou biping' (A comparison between the two Qing dynasty Dowager Empresses Xiaozhuang and Xiaoqin), *Gugong bowuyuan yuankan* (1982.3), (p.23).

63 Cleveland Museum of Art inv. no. 69.31.

64 Clark Worswick, p.22.

65 Jonathan D. Spence, *Emperor of China: Self-portrait of K'ang-Hsi* (London, 1974), p.157.

66 It has been pointed out that the dress descriptions and their symbolic meanings are one of the most effective artistic devices in the novelist's work. It must be borne in mind that he describes both archaic and contemporary Qing dress styles. See: 'The Role of Costume in Cao Xue-Qin's Novel "The Dream of the Red Chamber"',

translated from the Russian by Cecilia Shickman in *Tamkang Review,* 11 (Spring, 1981), 287-305 (pp.287-288).

67 Ye Mengzhu, p.178.

68 Cammann, *China's Dragon Robes,* pp.73-75 and pl.14.

69 *Zhongguo lidai fushi* (Chinese Historical Costume), separate list of captions in English, compiled by Shanghai shi xiqu xuexiao Zhongguo fuzhuang shi yanjiu zu (Shanghai, 1983), pp.245-249.

70 Shen Congwen, p.465 and p.468.

71 Ye Mengzhu, p.178.

72 *Changsha Mawangdui yi hao Han mu* (Han Tomb No. 1 at Mawangdui, Changsha) 2 vols, with English abstract (Peking, 1973), II, III, Krishna Riboud, 'Han Dynasty Specimens from Noin-Ula and Mawangdui in Looped-warp Weave', *Bulletin de liaison du centre international d'étude des textiles anciens,* 57-58 (1983), 16-38, Harold B. Burnham, *Chinese Velvets: A technical study,* Royal Ontario Museum (Toronto, 1959) pp.15-16.

73 Shen Congwen, p.441 and pp.466-467.

74 *chang shan* means 'long gown' and *cheong sam* is the Cantonese pronunciation of the characters.

75 *Zhongguo lidai fushi,* pp.316-317.

76 Little, *Intimate China,* p.124.

77 Juliet Bredon and Igor Mitrophanow, *The Moon Year* (Shanghai, 1927) p.127.

78 *Zhongguo lidai fushi,* p.307.

79 *Changsha Mawangdui...,* II, 88, 'Fuzhou shi bei jiao...' 1-16.

80 *Zhongguo lidai fushi,* p.264.

81 Mary Ellen Roach and Joanne B. Eicher, *The Visible Self: Perspectives on Dress* (New York, 1973), p.103.

82 Little, *Intimate China,* p.125.

83 Consul-General Hosie, p.37.

84 Rudolph P. Hommel, *China at Work: An Illustrated Record of the Primitive Industries of China's Masses whose Life is Toil, and thus an Account of Chinese Civilization* (New York, 1937 reprinted Cambridge Massachusetts, 1969), pp.190-192.

85 Lu Pu, *Designs of Chinese Indigo Batik* (Peking, 1981), Gernot Prunner, *Kunsthandwerk aus Guizhou, (China),* Hamburgisches Museum für Völkerkunde (Hamburg, 1983), pp.56-70.

86 Lady Hosie, p.286.

87 Ye Mengzhu, p.180.

88 A.S. Roe, *China as I saw it: A Woman's Letters from the Celestial Empire,* (London, 1910), p.314, John Henry Gray, *Walks in the City of Canton* (Hong Kong, 1875 reprinted San Francisco, 1974), pp.152-153.

89 *Silk: Replies from Commissioners of Customs...,* China, Maritime Customs II – Special Series: No.3 (Shanghai, 1881 reprinted 1917), p.64 and pp.98-104.

90 Gray, *Walks in the City of Canton,* p.263.

91 Natalis Rondot, *L'Industrie des Rubans de Soie,* Exposition Universelle de Vienne en 1873, second edition (Lyon, 1875), pp.42-43.

92 Consul-General Hosie, pp.73-74.

93 *Zhongguo lidai fushi,* pp.286-289.

94 Vollmer, p.23.

95 J. Thomson, *Illustrations of China and its People,* 4 vols (London, 1873-1874), II, pl.10,I and II preceding pl.10.

96 Liu E, *Lao Can you ji,* Renmin wenxue chubanshe ed. (Peking, 1979), p.95. English version in Liu T'ieh-yün, *The Travels of Lao Ts'an,* translated by Harold Shaddick (Ithaca and London, 1952), p.112.

97 The Victoria and Albert Museum has a pair of flower tubes made from chased and enamelled silver, inv. no. 1260-1883.

98 Lady Hosie, p.60.

99 A.C. Scott, *Chinese Costume in Transition* (New York, 1960), p.30 and p.32.

100 Thomson, I, pl.10 and preceding pl.10.

101 Couling, p.151.

102 Soothill, p.191.

103 Schuyler Cammann, 'The Symbolism of the Cloud Collar Motif', *The Art Bulletin,* 33 (1951), 1-9, Jessica Rawson, *Chinese Ornament: The Lotus and the Dragon,* British Museum (London, 1984), pp.132-138.

104 Gray, *Walks in the City of Canton,* p.235.

105 Consul-General Hosie, p.47.

106 Lady Hosie, p.150 and p.162.

107 Gray, *Walks in the City of Canton,* p.251.

108 Personal communication with the late Sir John Addis.

109 Little, *Intimate China,* pp.99-111.

110 Linda A. Pollock, *Forgotten Children: Parent-Child Relations from 1500-1900* (Cambridge, 1983), pp.48-49.

111 Lady Hosie, p.150.

112 Peter Osbeck, *Voyage to China and the East Indies,* 2 vols (London, 1771), I, 274.

113 Arthur Waley, *Yuan Mei: Eighteenth Century Chinese Poet* (London and New York, 1956), p.117.

114 Willard J. Peterson, *Bitter Gourd: Fang I-chih and the Impetus for Intellectual Change* (Yale, 1979), pp.161-162.

115 Shen Congwen, p.463.

116 *Zhongguo lidai fushi,* p.262.

117 'Kung I-chi' in *Selected Stories of Lu Hsun,* translated by Yang Hsien-yi and Gladys Yang (Peking, 1972), 19-24 (p.19).

118 Consul-General Hosie, p.37.

119 Shen Congwen, p.463.

120 Julia Hutt, 'Chinese fans and fans from China', in *Fans from the East,* Fan Circle/Victoria and Albert Museum (London, 1978), pp.27-35 (pp.29-35).

121 Scott, p.40.

122 *Zhongguo lidai fushi,* pp.300-301.

123 *Zhongguo lidai fushi,* p.312.

124 Lady Hosie, p.83.

125 Arthur P. Wolf, 'Chinese Kinship and Mourning Dress' in *Family and Kinship in Chinese Society,* edited by Maurice Freedman, Studies in Chinese Society (Stanford, 1970), pp.189-207 (p.189 and p.197).

126 Mrs Arnold Foster, *In the Valley of the Yangtse* (London, 1899), p.47.

127 Liu E, *Lao Can you ji,* p.168, *The Travels of Lao Ts'an,* translated by Shaddick, p.194.

128 Foster, p.47.

129 Lady Susan Townley, *My Chinese Notebook* (London, 1904), pp.183-184.

130 Roach and Eicher, p.84.

131 Lady Hosie, p.212.

132 S. Wells Williams, *The Middle Kingdom,* 2 vols (New York and London, 1845), II, 34 and 30.

133 Consul-General Hosie, p.38.

134 Consul-General Hosie, p.85, John Henry Gray, *China: A History of the Laws, Manners, and Customs of the People,* 2 vols (London, 1878), II, 144.

135 Liu E, *Lao Can you ji,* p.71, *The Travels of Lao Ts'an,* translated Shaddick, p.84.

136 *Zhongguo lidai fushi*, pp.300-301.

137 Osbeck, I, 269.

138 Gray, *Walks in the City of Canton*, p.286.

139 *Zhongguo lidai fushi*, pp.294-296.

140 Consul-General Hosie, pp.30-31, Hommel, p.192.

141 Cao Xueqin, II, p.375.

142 Edward T. Williams, 'The Worship of Lei Tsu, Patron Saint of Silk Workers', *Journal of the North China Branch of the Royal Asiatic Society*, 66 (1935), 1-14 (p.2).

143 Gray, *Walks in the City of Canton*, p.617.

144 Edward T. Williams, p.1.

145 E-tu Zen Sun, 'Sericulture and Silk Textile Production in Ch'ing China', in *Economic Organization in Chinese Society*, edited by W.E. Willmott, Studies in Chinese Society (Stanford, 1972), pp.79-108 (p.79).

146 Robert Fortune, *A Residence Among the Chinese* (London, 1857), p.357.

147 *Zhongguo sichou/Chinese Silk*, China Silk Corporation (n.p., 1982), p.142.

148 Fortune, p.353.

149 *Silk*, pp.46-49.

150 Fortune, pp.344-345.

151 E-tu Zen Sun, p.88.

152 Fortune, p.367.

153 *Zhongguo sichou/Chinese Silk*, p.110.

154 Consul-General Hosie, pp.42-43 and pp.62-67.

155 Li Renpu, *Zhongguo gudai fangzhi shigao* (Draft History of Ancient Chinese Weaving) (Changsha, 1983), p.239.

156 *Chinese Repository*, 4 (August, 1835), p.185.

157 Chen Juanjuan, p.93.

158 Cao Xueqin, III, 215.

159 Simon B. Heilesen, 'Southern Journey', *Bulletin of the Museum of Far Eastern Antiquities, Stockholm*, 52 (1980), 89-144 (p.108).

160 Song Boyin, 'Suzhou Qingdai zhishu diaocha jianbao' (Report on an investigation of the Qing dynasty weaving office at Suzhou), *Wenwu cankao ziliao* (1958.9), 32-34.

161 E-tu Zen Sun, p.100.

162 Little, *Intimate China*, p.349.

163 *Silk*, p.33, p.36, pp.62-64, pp.83-84 and p.143.

164 E-tu Zen Sun, pp.79-80.

165 Dorothy K. Burnham, *Warp and Weft: A Textile Terminology*, Royal Ontario Museum (Toronto, 1980), pp.124-125.

166 *Silk*, p.106.

167 Roe, p.88, Gray, *Walks in the City of Canton*, p.468.

168 Qian Yong, *Fu Yuan Cong Hua* (General Talks from the Garden of Clogs) Qingdai shiliao biji congkan, 2 vols (Peking, 1979), I, 324.

169 Roe, pp.318-319.

170 Hommell, p.195 and fig.284.

171 Museum of Mankind, London inv. no.1896-66.

172 Hommell, pp.193-200, figs.282-283 and fig.285.

173 Lady Hosie, p.152.

174 *Silk*, pp.90-92.

175 E-tu Zen Sun, pp.94-96, Li Renpu, pp.254-255.

176 Shen Fu, p.25.

177 Soothill, pp.181-182.

178 *Silk*, p.75.

179 Cao Xueqin, I, 108, III, 256, IV, 249.

180 Rozsika Parker, *The Subversive Stitch: Embroidery and the Making of the Feminine* (London, 1984), p.132.

181 Edwin Joshua Dukes, *Everyday Life in China: Scenes along River and Road in Fuh-kien* (London, 1887), pp.30-31.

182 For methods of printing and tracing as applied to watercolours see Craig Clunas, *Chinese Export Watercolours*, Victoria and Albert Museum Far Eastern Series (London, 1984), pp.73-74.

183 Mrs Archibald Christie, *Samplers and Stitches: A Handbook of the Embroiderer's Art* (London, 1920), p.10.

184 Gray, *Walks in the City of Canton*, p.290.

185 *Chinese Hands*, edited by Peter Thompson (n.p., n.d.), p.13.

186 Christie, pp.67-68, Zhu Feng, *Zhongguo ci xiu ji fa yen jiu* (The Art of Embroidery in China) (Shanghai, 1957), pp.28-29, Wang Yarong, *Zhongguo minjian ci xiu* (Chinese Folk Embroidery), Zhongguo wenhua yishu congshu (Hong Kong, 1985), p.139.

187 The name canvas implies an evenly-woven cloth of strength and firmness. It does not refer to a specific weave or fabric. See *Textile Terms and Definitions*, edited by Carolyn A. Farnfield and P.J. Alvey, The Textile Institute (Manchester, 1975), p.28.

188 Christie, p.115 and p.117.

189 This is sometimes called découpé work or underlaid appliqué in the West. See Mary Thomas, *Book of Embroidery* (London, 1936), p.15, Irene Emery, *The Primary Structures of Fabrics: An Illustrated Classification*, The Textile Museum (Washington, 1966 reprinted 1980), p.251.

190 Alan Priest, *Imperial Robes and Textiles of the Chinese Court*, Minneapolis Institute of Arts (Minneapolis, 1943), Alan Priest,

Costumes from the Forbidden City, Metropolitan Museum of Art (New York, 1945), Helen E. Fernald, *Chinese Court Costumes,* Royal Ontarion Museum of Archaeology (Toronto, 1946), Vollmer, *In the Presence of the Dragon Throne.*

191 Shen Congwen, p.442.

192 Painting of Chinese official with his son in the National Museum of Denmark, Copenhagen inv. no. B.4812, *Palastmuseum Peking: Schätze aus der Verbotenen Stadt,* p.146.

193 Schuyler Cammann, *Spansk korkåpa av kinesiskt broderi,* with English summary, Malmö Museum, katalog no. 310 (Malmö, 1974).

194 Schuyler Cammann, 'A Rare Ming Textile in Sweden', *Archives of the Chinese Arts Society of America,* 17(1963), 32-37.

195 Wei Gongqin, 'Jieshao jijian chaopao yi liao' (Introducing some lengths of material for court robes), *Wenwu cankao ziliao* (1958.9), 24-27.

196 Cammann, *China's Dragon Robes,* p.58 note 5.

197 *Portrait Paintings of the Ming and Qing Dynasties,* pls. 9, 11, 12 and 18, Cammann, *China's Dragon Robes,* p.17 note 30.

198 c.f. another altered red robe in the National Museum of Denmark, Copenhagen inv. no. R. VII. 701.

199 Rose Kerr, *Chinese Ceramics: Porcelain of the Qing Dynasty (1644-1911),* Victoria and Albert Museum Far Eastern Series (London, 1986), chapter 4 dealing with marks on porcelain.

200 *Exhibition of Treasures of Imperial Palace: A Picture Album* (Peking, 1981), pl.9.

201 *Gugong bowuyuan zang Qingdai zhi xiu tuan hua tu'an* (Designs of Qing dynasty embroidered roundels in the Palace Museum) (Peking, 1959), pl.18.

202 William Crookes, *A Practical Handbook of Dyeing and Calico Printing* (London, 1874), K.G. Ponting, *A Dictionary of Dyes and Dyeing* (London, 1980).

203 Cammann, *China's Dragon Robes,* p.62 note 16 and p.63 note 17.

204 Fashion plates and magazines, an obvious source for historians of European dress, are rare for China. Only a few are known to the author e.g. Tian Xu Wo-sheng, *Shanghai shi zhuang tu yong* (Shanghai Women's Fashion Book) (Shanghai, 1915 reprinted Taipei, 1968).

205 Mrs Archibald Little, *Round About My Peking Garden* (London, 1905), pp.102-103.

206 *With Gordon in China: Letters from Thomas Lyster,* edited by E.A. Lyster (London, 1891), p.250.

Select Bibliography

Schuyler Cammann, *China's Dragon Robes* (New York, 1952).

Walter A. Fairservis, Jr., *Costumes of the East*, The American Museum of Natural History (Riverside, 1971).

A.C. Scott, *Chinese Costume in Transition* (New York, 1960).

John E. Vollmer, *In the Presence of the Dragon Throne: Ch'ing Dynasty Costume (1644-1911) in the Royal Ontario Museum* (Toronto, 1977).

Zhou Xun and Gao Chunming, *5000 Years of Chinese Costumes* (Hong Kong, 1987).

Index

Bold type indicates pages of plates for which no other reference is given; other plates mentioned will be found under one of the pages already given for that entry.